JEFFREY S. HUTCHINS
P. O. BOX 5272
TRENTON, N.J. 08638

D1107363

SOUND IN
THE THEATRE

SOUND IN THE THEATRE

Harold Burris-Meyer, Vincent Mallory and Lewis S. Goodfriend

Revised, expanded edition

THEATRE ARTS BOOKS

New York

Dedicated

to

DOROTHEA MALLORY

Copyright © 1959 by Radio Magazines, Inc.
Copyright © 1979 by Harold Burris-Meyer, Dorothea Mallory
and Lewis S. Goodfriend
Library of Congress Catalog Card No. 78 660 64
ISBN 0-87830-157-7
Designed by Bernard Schleifer
Manufactured in the United States of America

Published by Theatre Arts Books
153 Waverly Place
New York, New York zip 10014

All rights reserved. Except for brief passages quoted in
a newspaper, magazine, radio, or television review, no part
of this book may be reproduced in any form or by any means,
electronic or mechanical, including photocopying and recording,
or by any information storage and retrieval system, without
permission in writing from the Publishers.

CONTENTS

FOREWORD

This BOOK has to do with sound as an artist's medium. It will help the reader analyze the dramatic values which can be achieved through the control of sound during a performance. It sets forth the devices and techniques by which this control is exercised. They apply to all types of stages.

Since the original publication of *Sound in the Theatre* in 1959 there has been a growing recognition of the dramatic potential of sound control. The use of electronic sound-reproducing apparatus in the theatre has become well-nigh universal, but these devices, lamentably, seldom contribute to the effectiveness of a performance. Voices are amplified (and often distorted) in theatres where performers a generation ago needed no such electronic crutch. Special effects are produced from tape recordings when mechanical devices may do the job better and more cheaply. Sound levels in some productions are raised so high that they can cause permanent hearing loss. The subtle and imaginative control of any substantial part of the audio component of a show has progressed little, and books and articles dealing with sound in the theatre neglect, to a large extent, such factors basic to the control of sound as architecture, scenery, the structure of the human voice and ear, and psycho-acoustics.

But now the function of the sound designer is accepted, and the need for at least one person to be responsible for whatever is undertaken in sound control during a performance is recognized. With responsibility thus fixed, the control of sound may well improve—as did the visual component of shows with the advent of the lighting designer.

The techniques herein described have been developed and tested in actual production on and off Broadway for many years. It is impossible to list and thank individually all of the people who have helped us in the preparation of this book. Those whose names are mentioned in the text are only a very few of them. We are grateful to the playwrights and composers, the producers, directors, maestros, conductors, actors, singers, dancers, instrumentalists, designers, theatre technicians, and technical directors who have worked with us on the productions in which we experimented with, and many times achieved, an effective control of sound. Manufacturers have lent us equipment and counsel; the press has treated us generously; Actors' Equity and the International Alliance of Theatrical Stage Employees, the stagehands' union, have smoothed our path; and the Rockefeller Foundation, the Research Corporation, the Stevens Research Foundation, and generous individuals have supplied funds. Most of all we are indebted to the engineers, musicians, and theatre people who made up our research staff at Stevens Institute of Technology. We gratefully acknowledge the assistance of all of them.

Vincent Mallory, the distinguished acoustician and coauthor of the first edition of *Sound in the Theatre*, died shortly after it was published. We have tried in this second edition to retain his wisdom and something of his felicitous style.

HAROLD BURRIS-MEYER
LEWIS S. GOODFRIEND

New York, 1978

CHAPTER I

BACKGROUND

'Tis not enough no harshness gives offense
The sound must seem an echo to the sense.

Alexander Pope
ESSAY ON CRITICISM

SOUND is an essential element of almost every theatrical form. Even those performances usually thought of as silent are not silent in fact. The pantomime has a reader or a musical accompaniment. The ballet is seldom better than its music. The silent motion picture evoked stereotyped mood music, and a robust style of piano playing. The ENTRANCE OF THE GLADIATORS march is indispensable to the elephant act, and the seals work to Walteufel.

As in the case of the *visual* component of the performance, the usefulness and effectiveness of sound are measured by the extent to which it is controlled. To exploit the visual component, the theatre has adopted scenery, the mask, the raked floor, the curved seat-rows in the house, stage machinery, lighting instruments, and systems of lighting control.

The effort to control the *auditory* component has brought forth resonating kettles placed at the back of the theatre, mechanical noisemaking and effect machines, the roof and the ceiling over the *auditorium*. (The derivation of the word is significant.) The physical form of the theatre no less than the form of the presentation has arisen from the necessities of seeing and hearing. The twentieth century has brought a vast increase in acoustical knowledge, and electronic and mechanical facilities for the control of sound. The application of these facilities to the needs of the theatre is the subject of this book.

THE THEATRE

Theatre in this book is broadly defined. It means not only the conventional playhouse with an audience and a performance, but any instance in which a sound is produced by man or instrument and in one operation travels to the listener's ear, and where between source and hearer, control may be applied. Theatre includes the opera and the Music Hall, the runway, the midway, Carnegie Hall, *son et lumière*.

While this definition of theatre excludes television and radio transmission, since there control is divided, it does include that portion of the program which is projected to a live audience in the studio. It includes sound amplification in night-clubs and vaudeville; sound for voice and music reinforcement for churches, halls, and auditoriums; sound reinforcement and control for open-air productions, the playhouse, the concert stage, and the opera. Most of the illustrative material will be drawn from the applications of sound control to productions of the legitimate theatre and the opera, where the demands are most severe. The principles on which such applications are based serve for all other theatrical forms.

CHARACTERISTICS OF SOUND

Sound, or that part of sound which is the province of this book, is a series of pressure waves (alternate compressions and rarefactions) in the air. It has long been customary to compare the spreading of these waves to the circular expanding ripples which result when a stone is dropped into water. This, however, is only partly true. The surface of the water shows us the expanding waves in but two dimensions whereas in air the sound-wave front propagates as a continually expanding sphere unless it meets an obstacle.

Sound has two basic characteristics, intensity and frequency. *Intensity* is a measure of the amplitude of the pressure waves. It is interpreted by the ear in terms of *loudness*. The greater the size of the waves, the more power they transmit, the louder the sound. *Intensity*, a physical dimension, and *loudness*, a subjective measure of sensation, do not bear an unvarying relation to each other, but intensity is the principal physical factor controlling the sensation of loudness. Intensity level is measured in decibels, (dB), the unit being the logarithm of the ratio of the sound power per unit area (intensity) to an arbitrary intensity which is 10^{-12} watts per square meter (10^{-12} W/m^2).

Frequency is a measure of the number of pressure waves per second. The unit is Hertz (Hz). Frequency is interpreted by the ear as *pitch*. The more pressure waves (cycles) per second, the greater the frequency and the higher the pitch.

A complex sound (almost all sounds are) consists of waves

containing numerous frequencies at different intensities. Such a sound is said to have a spectrum. Sounds whose frequencies are integral multiples of a fundamental are *harmonics* of that fundamental note or, in musical terminology, overtones.

A sound wave travels in air at moderate temperatures at a speed of about 1130 feet per second. As the series of waves proceeds from its source, the actor's mouth, for example, a portion goes directly to the ear of the listener, some is first reflected by scenery, proscenium, walls or ceiling. The angle of reflection is equal to the angle of incidence.

Some sound is absorbed in soft surfaces, hangings, clothes, or in the air itself, and never reaches the listener. Hard surfaces reflect sound, soft surfaces absorb it. The unit of absorption is the sabin (s), which is equal to the amount of absorption provided by one square foot of open window where the sound goes out and doesn't come back.

Reverberation is the persistence of sound when it is reflected about in an enclosed space. The measure of reverberation is the time it takes the sound intensity to drop to 1 millionth of its intensity (60 dB) after the sound source has stopped. In churches and coliseums, the reverberation time is often so long that the sounds of speech overlap and blur.

SCOPE

Sound in the theatre has the following functions:
1. To transmit the human voice in speech or song (adequate audibility is always the first requisite).
2. To establish locale (bird songs, traffic noises).
3. To establish atmosphere (wind and rain).
4. To create and sustain mood (combinations of devices used for locale and atmosphere; distortion of speech; soft music).
5. As an independent arbitrary emotional stimulus (music, non-associative sounds).
6. As an actor (the voice of the LIVING NEWSPAPER).
7. To reveal character (the unspoken aside).
8. To advance the plot (sound bridges between scenes or episodes).

These functions may be undertaken singly, in combination, independently, or counterpointing or reinforcing their equivalents in the visual component of the show. Their full accomplishment requires that it shall be possible for the audience to hear *any sound from any source, or no source, or a moving source with any frequency spectrum or intensity from any apparent distance, in any apparent direction, and with any desired reverberant quality*.

LIMITATIONS

Traditional forms of presentation undertake no such elaborate control of sound as is here listed. This circumstance is not the fault of the playwright; Shakespeare demands all that

the best modern techniques can provide. It comes about basically because the showman is seldom technically competent, and the technician often does not know show business.

Only a few of the theatres built in this country before World War II were designed with any thought of acoustics. Very few turned out to be better than acoustically tolerable. Many have undergone various types of architectural alteration to overcome acoustic limitations. No attempt to improve a bad structure has produced as good a theatre or as cheaply as can be achieved with integral acoustical design. The public address system too often is used as a crutch, with which an attempt is made to compensate for bad theatre planning. In this use, the public address system is never quite successful, and the performance suffers.

In that part of sound control that is electronic, radio broadcast is the parent art. As a result, much of the sound operation in the theatre is a recognizable offspring. Many

SOUND LEVEL: Decibels	SOUND INTENSITY
130	Threshold of pain
120	Jet take-off at 2500 feet. Hammering on steel plate
110	Thunder (the thunder drum is well below this
100	Subway express train passing Large Symphony Orchestra (forte) Niagara Falls, loudest part Lion's roar in reverberant lion house
90	Heavy street traffic
80	Voice of trained actor at 3 feet
70	Noisy office Conversation at 3 feet
60	Background noise, chiefly subway rumble, in Carnegie Hall Quiet suburban street
50	Soft music (background for the renunciation scene in CAMILLE)
40	Average residence Ambient level in empty theatre
30	
20	Quiet whisper
10	
0	Threshold of hearing

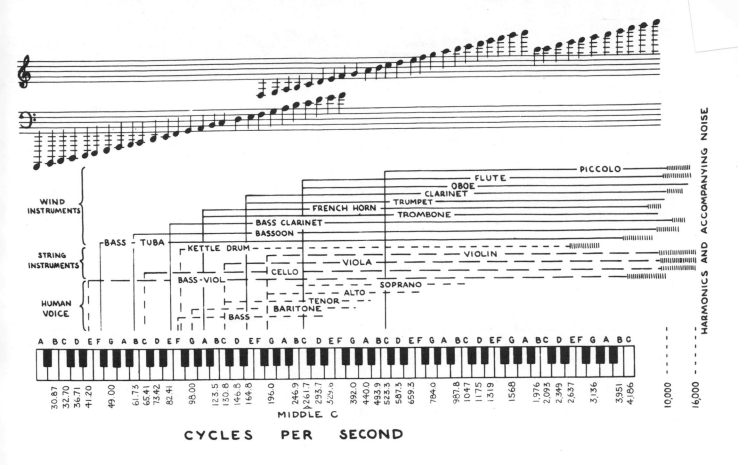

Useful Frequency Range of Sound.

practices have been developed in broadcast which are not suitable to sound control in the theatre.

One such practice is that of secondary monitoring, in which audible material projected to an audience is monitored by means of headphones or a loudspeaker backstage or in an acoustically treated room. A cardinal rule of sound control is that *the operator must be so stationed that he hears what the audience hears, directly.*

Another such practice, however, which is no longer respected in broadcast studios, is wrong microphone position and distance. The layman believes that the microphone is to be treated as a telephone. This misconception is fostered by performers carrying a microphone and towing a cable about the stage and crooners hanging for support upon the microphone stand. Many microphone amplifier systems distort badly when a respectful distance is not maintained.

On the current vestigial vaudeville stage, subtle and delicate reinforcement is often neglected and the voice of the singer is merely increased in intensity. This is readily understandable as a necessity for spent young ladies who sing with dance bands. In the case of the trained singer or speaker, inappropriate loudness and disproportionate emphasis of low frequencies result in an unreal stentorian voice, when suave, understandable speech is required.

Sound reinforcement suffers not only from faults in pickup and operation, but often from installation of equipment with no regard for the acoustics of the theatre or the way people hear. A too common fault is hanging loudspeakers either side of the proscenium, a practice which decreases the intelligibility of speech. And the attempted cure—raising the level—only makes it worse. The precept that the audience must never be conscious of the sound system cannot be ignored without downgrading the performance.

Styles of acting have changed. Since Nazimova played an entire scene with her back to the audience (in BELLADONNA), less accomplished players have cultivated intimate style while neglecting the development of adequate skill in voice projection. Speech and song whose intensity and definition are adequate in motion pictures and television will often not get beyond the sixth row in theatres. Electronic devices cannot compensate for lack of training and discipline but are, and will probably continue to be, used to prop up the mediocre performer.

In approaching the problem of control of sound, it is apparent that the last part in the transmission is the least controllable, that is, the ear itself. The ear's characteristics are, nevertheless, a determining factor in the planning of all sound control.

HISTORY OF CONTROL

The principal problem of architectural acoustics—that of making it possible for all the people in the auditorium to hear distinctly—has been solved since the turn of the century. Two outstanding examples are the Kleinhans Music Hall in Buffalo and the Listening Room at the Bell Telephone Laboratories, Murray Hill, New Jersey. Few large legitimate theatres in the United States completely satisfy the audibility requirements. The nature, scope, subtlety, and variety of acoustical demands imposed on a building by legitimate and operatic production are too little understood by acoustical planners.

Electronic control was successfully applied to the problem of making the motion picture talk in THE JAZZ SINGER (Warner Brothers, 1927). Electronic control was first applied in the legitimate theatre for a specialty number in THE GRAND STREET FOLLIES of the same year.

The problem of using and controlling orchestral music without an orchestra and employing dynamic range greater than an orchestra could supply as an essential element in a multimedia production was undertaken in 1930 in George P. Baker's pageant, CONTROL, produced for the fiftieth anniversary of the American Society of Mechanical Engineers in the Stevens Theatre, Stevens Institute of Technology, Hoboken, New Jersey.

In 1933, the Bell Telephone Laboratories demonstrated three-channel transmission. The sound—in this case orchestral music—was played in one theatre and reproduced in another with such fidelity that the audience accepted the reproduced music as the real thing. The system retained, in the reproduction, the position of the various instruments in the orchestra, made possible the apparent movement of the source of sound, and provided a dynamic range considerably in excess of that which the actual instruments could provide. In 1940, recording and reproduction were added to stereophonic transmission and demonstrated first at Carnegie Hall. This system in modified form was soon adopted for wide-screen motion pictures.

Control of spectrum, distance, direction, movement, and dynamics was applied to legitimate production in a demonstration, THE SOUND SHOW, at the Stevens Theatre, 1934, and became an essential element of every production of the Federal Theatre's LIVING NEWSPAPER.

The electronic control of acoustic conditions of the stage was first used in 1940 at a concert in which Paul Robeson appeared as soloist with the Philadelphia Orchestra at Carnegie Hall. This technique (the Acoustic Envelope) plus selective

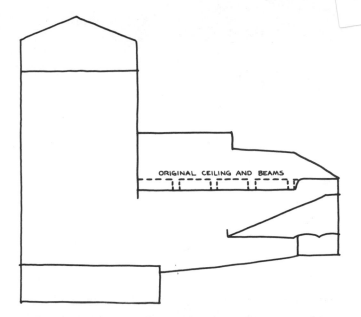

ANTA Playhouse showing reconstruction to improve acoustics. Ceiling was lowered to reduce volume and eliminate beams. Ceiling under balcony was sloped to improve sound distribution.

control of backstage acoustics and elements of the opera as heard by the audience was employed at the Metropolitan Opera during the seasons of 1940-41 and 1941-42.

In 1941, the SECOND SOUND SHOW at the Stevens Theatre demonstrated the control and use in legitimate and operatic productions of the remade voice, subsonics, and reverberation.

Research and development projects, supported by the Rockefeller Foundation, The Research Corporation, The Stevens Research Foundation, and the Bell Telephone Laboratories, achieved the progressive development of sound control here noted.

The National Defense Research project, THE EFFECT OF SOUND ON MAN, undertaken at Stevens in 1941, produced the term Psycho-Acoustics, and found intriguing and immensely profitable military uses for psycho-acoustical phenomena. Instrumentation (the Encabulator) developed later under the U.S. Office of Education, made it possible to measure the effect of auditory stimuli.

Though there is ample room for further refinement, facilities for sound control are now adequate to the needs of any show. It is possible for the showman to use sound as an arbitrary independent means for stimulating predictable involuntary audience reaction; to engender by auditory means that emotional flux which will make it easy for the audience to suspend disbelief, to laugh, to weep, to believe in something which would have seemed the veriest fancy when first the curtain went up.

With complete control extended to the auditory component of the performance, that component becomes perhaps more generally useful than the visual component. You can shut your eyes but the sound comes out and gets you.

A page from the three channel stereophonic recording script for the duel scene in Rostand's CYRANO DE BERGERAC. All sounds in the scene—the ring of the blades, crowd noises, footfalls, the actors' lines—were arranged as a musical pattern. The heightened emotional impact, conventionally brought about by a musical accompaniment, was thus achieved without the artificiality of using conventional musical instruments.

CHAPTER II

HEARING AND PSYCHO-ACOUSTICS

THE COMMON expression "eye and ear entertainment" as a synonym for a musical show aptly defines the aim of the production. The ear is the receiver and critic for all sound in the show. To make the most effective production, it is necessary to know the ear, its capabilities, limitations, and the psychological responses to sound.

THE EAR

For the purposes of this discussion the term *the ear* will include not only the physiological receptor but also the elements of the nerve network associated with it which are involved in the analysis, integration, and interpretation of sound. The external ear collects sound of all audible frequencies with reasonably similar efficiency. The sound wave entering the ear sets into vibration the eardrum and the mechanical linkage, hammer, anvil, and stirrup. The linkage forms a mechanical amplifier which increases slightly the amplitude of sound waves striking the eardrum and transmits that vibration to the base of the cochlea. The cochlea contains an incompressible fluid which carries the vibration impressed upon it to all portions of the inner surface of the cochlea in undiminished intensity and unchanged frequency relationship. The bundle of nerves which carry auditory sensations to the brain terminates in the cochlea. Fibrous hair-like nerve endings are distributed throughout the length of this organ. They respond to discrete frequencies depending upon the resonance of the cochlea and the length of the fibres.

As may be seen, the ear is a mechanical device, subject to the same acoustic laws which apply to all structures and mechanisms including, notably, resonance of various portions and groups of parts and various forms of distortion incident thereto.

FREQUENCY RANGE

The typical ear responds to frequencies as indicated in the accompanying chart between 16 and 16,000 Hz (Hertz). As a matter of fact, it is possible to have a sensation of tone at frequencies considerably higher, perhaps as high as 30,000 Hz, but in most cases the threshold of audibility for frequencies above 20,000 Hz is considerably above the threshold of pain. That is, the sound must be raised to such an intensity that the hearer suffers considerable pain before he is able to identify a sensation of tone. The hearing of older people or people exposed to intense noise or gunfire for long periods deteriorates through loss of sensitivity to higher frequency sounds, and the person who at age 60 can hear more than 10,000 Hz is the exception. The sensation of tone, however, appears to exist even when tests indicate that the ear is not effective as a receptor for the frequency in question. One musician past middle age, whom tests showed to be deaf to frequencies over 6000 Hz, used to complain when the reproduced music to which he was listening was cut off above 8000 Hz.

Also frequencies below the audible range have been demonstrated to be effective in the theatre. A 12-cycle inaudible note was introduced at drum-beat cadence at the rise of the curtain in THE EMPEROR JONES (Stevens Theatre, 1941). This impressed the rhythm on the audience before the drum was heard and induced a degree of awe and apprehension not equalled by any other means when the drum was first heard.

There is a paradoxical situation, for at low frequencies where the ear is less sensitive to intensity alone, it is more

The ear judges as equally loud all the frequencies on any single curve e.g. on the 20 Phon equal loudness curve 18 dB at 5000 Hz sounds as loud as 74 dB at 30 Hz.

sensitive to intensity change. This results in the natural inclination of the listener to desire bass increase when he listens to music reproduction at low level. In theatre application, this characteristic makes it possible to convince the hearer that he is listening to a receding band or effective sound when over-all intensity, for technical reasons, is reduced only slightly. The reduction of the low-frequency part of the spectrum gives the auditory impression of increasing distance.

ANALYSIS

As may be seen from its structure, the ear can hear and transmit to the brain the sensation of many frequencies simultaneously, and it is possible to sort out and identify the various frequencies simultaneously presented. At a single instant, the musicians in an orchestra may be playing as many as a dozen different simultaneous notes, and the listener even without benefit of score, without knowing the piece or with no theoretical knowledge of harmony can pick out most of the notes. And, by virtue of the different spectra of the instruments involved, he can also identify the individual instruments.

INTEGRATION

Not only does the ear analyze the sounds presented to it, but it integrates masses of auditory data. In most enclosed spaces the louder the sound the longer the reverberation. The

THE WELL KNOWN FLETCHER-MUNSON CURVES

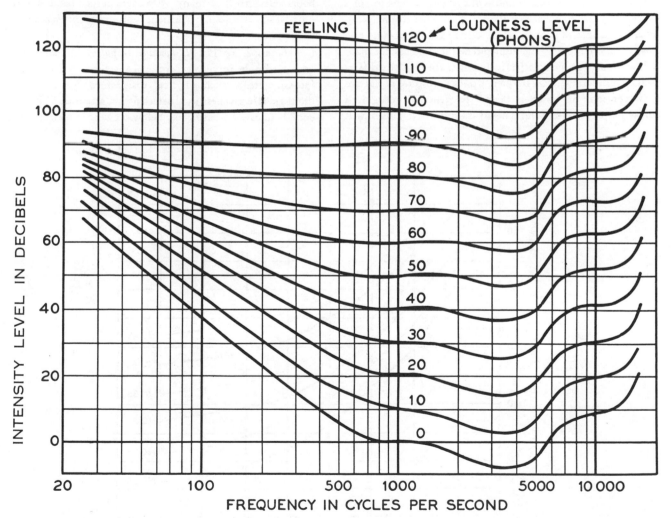

ear therefore associates long reverberation with loudness. When two sounds of equal intensity are presented, one having a long reverberation and the other little or none, the sound with the longer reverberation will be interpreted as the louder of the two. The technique of making a sound appear to be louder than it actually is has obvious theatrical applications.

The ear is accustomed to hearing sounds which have a regular harmonic structure. If a sound consisting of a harmonic series is presented to the ear, the ear hears all the elements of the series. If some of the elements are omitted, the ear supplies them. This is illustrated by the elephant bell whose low strike-note is entirely subjective—it does not exist in the air but is supplied by the ear as the low end of the actual harmonic series given out by the bell.

MASKING

The functions of analysis and integration have their limitations, of course. A loud sound will prevent the hearing of a less-loud sound of another frequency. Most effective masking occurs in the case of a low-pitched sound masking a sound two octaves or more higher. The high-pitched sound does not mask the low-pitched sound so effectively unless the intensity differential is considerable. Low frequency pulses projected at the rate of 10 per second, which is below the generally recognized audible frequency range and is heard as a series of impulses, will

mask all audible sound within a few dB of the masking intensity. Overture and entr'acte music, in addition to its primary task of inducing mood progression, does much in some theatres to preserve the audience's good temper by masking backstage noise incident to scene shifts.

DYNAMICS

As stated in Chapter I, the zero point on the decibel scale is a sound intensity usually too weak to be heard by the ear under the most favorable listening conditions and at the frequency to which the ear is most sensitive. The noise level in the quietest theatres is below the 30 dB NC curve. With an audience present, it is hard to find moments at which the noise level is less than 40 dB. The ear can tolerate intensities as high as 120 dB for very short periods of time. However, these high intensities, if repeated or prolonged, will induce temporary hearing loss, and tinnitus, both of which usually disappear within 24 hours. Nevertheless, many performers in rock bands and rock musical shows sustain permanent hearing loss, often as much as 50 percent.

Intensities over 110 dB should be scrupulously avoided and 100 employed only in very exceptional instances. Sounds of such intensity create such physical discomfort that they forfeit dramatic effectiveness by distracting the attention of the audience. Sounds of intensity just below the range which engenders

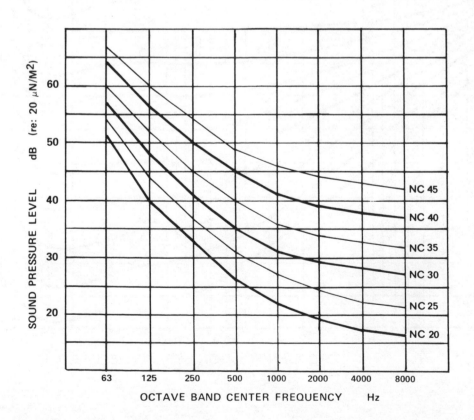

discomfort are theatrically extremely effective. This was demonstrated spectacularly in the scene of Brünnhilde's immolation from GOTTERDAMMERUNG conducted by Leopold Stokowski for the first multi-channel recording system developed by the Bell Telephone Laboratories. (Chapter V, Problem 6B.)

Theatrical use of high intensity sound in combination with reverberation control was first demonstrated in a recorded performance of the TOCATTA IN F from Widor's 5th Organ Symphony. (Chapter V, Problems 3 and 15.)

Differences in frequency are interpreted by the ear to a certain extent as differences in intensity, and vice versa; i.e., if two sounds of equal intensity but different frequency are presented, the listener will pick the high-pitched sound as being the louder of the two. When two sounds of the same frequency but different intensities are presented in sequence, the listener will identify the louder of the two sounds as having the higher frequency.

LOCALIZATION

Due to the shape of the head, the conformation of the outer ear, and the distance between ears, it is possible to localize sound within perhaps 15 deg. in azimuth. This is done by turning the head to the position at which sound is heard with equal intensity and at the same time by both ears. Time difference is an important element in localization. Sound from one side reaches one ear before it reaches the other. Therefore a *PA loudspeaker must, except in the case of a low-level system, be approximately in the same vertical plane as the source*, or the illusion of reality is destroyed. The mediocrity of many concerts in which loudspeakers at either side of the proscenium are used is accounted for by this technical error.

The ear is as inaccurate in altitude as it is precise in appreciating direction in azimuth. It is almost impossible to tell the difference in source between the sound coming from directly in front of the listener or 60 deg. above that point. In Radio

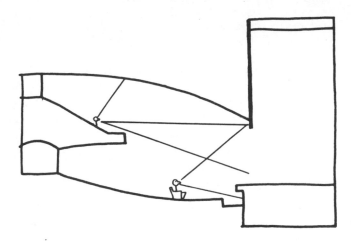

Localization, Altitude: The listener cannot tell whether the sound is coming from the ceiling, above the proscenium, the stage, or the orchestra pit, as long as it is in the vertical plane of the apparent source.

City Music Hall most of the sound from the stage show is projected from loudspeakers above the proscenium but is accepted as coming from the performers.

Sounds coming from behind the listener or above him are identifiable as to source not because of the source itself but because of reflections of the sound from walls, floor, and so on. Sound which has a general source, i.e., comes to the listener at approximately equal intensity from all about him, may be interpreted by him as coming from nowhere, as being generated within his own head, as surrounding him, or as coming from a localized source, depending upon what visual indication or spoken suggestion of the location of sound source is given him, or upon what seems logical in view of the nature of the sound.

DOPPLER EFFECT

When a sound source is moving toward the listener, the frequency appears to be higher than when the sound source is stationary. This is because each succeeding wave has a shorter distance to travel from source to hearer. Thus more waves per second are received by the hearer than are sent out by the source. As a sound source passes the hearer, the frequency and pitch drop. Since each succeeding wave of the receding source has a longer travel than the one before it, the hearer receives fewer waves per second than the source generates. These phenomena are easily noticed in the passing of an aircraft or racing car. The ear's readiness to interpret pitch change as change of distance is theatrically useful, especially in combination with other phenomena such as direction. This was effectively demonstrated in the Federal Theatre production HIGHLIGHTS OF 1935 in which the sound of an airplane was brought in from a distance in auditory perspective, circled over the audience, and carried to a landing far upstage.

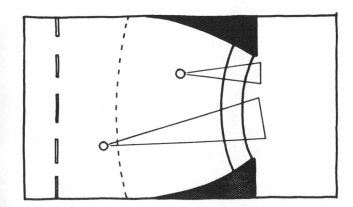

Localization, Azimuth: The listener can locate the source of sound within a few degrees.

PSYCHO-ACOUSTICS

Many characteristics of sound have theatrical uses irrespective and often independent of the meaningful content or the circumstances in which they are employed. The skill with which they are used is often the measure of the effectiveness of the piece. It is impossible here to more than suggest a few. Their discovery and use are the province of the artist.

Cyclic Characteristics

Cyclic characteristics of sound appear in music as rhythm and as vibrato. Vibrato in the singing voice is most pleasing at the rate of 6 to 6.5 cycles per second. The organ vibrato ranges from 6 to 12 cycles per second, depending on the type of organ and the individual stops.

After a sound source has stopped, the decay may often have a cyclic characteristic.

A classical demonstration of the involuntary physical response to a cyclic sound stimulus is to whistle a tune in time to one's pulse rate, then arbitrarily increase the tempo of the tune and observe that the pulse rate increases also.

The theatrical applications of this phenomenon are obvious—reverberant footsteps of the hangman in the corridor, the drum in EMPEROR JONES, the brainstorm in THE ADDING MACHINE.

Non-associative but demonstrably effective cyclic phenomena possibly used with flicker in light (7 to 20 cps: most effective at 9 cps) have still to be exploited in the theatre.

Startle

For an appreciable instant all startled humans act alike. This fact is exploited by the showman as a device for creating tension and inducing that emotional flux which is the mark of a good show. A sound which has a steep wave front and is projected at high intensity has an appreciable physiological effect upon those it touches. The viscera-tightening episode is often dependent upon this phenomenon.

Musical Idioms

There is a reasonable unanimity of association between certain types of music and specific moods. There is no accepted technical system of musical classification which describes the discrete elements which make up mood despite the obvious need for such a system in functional music. However, the low lights and soft music evoke a standard response, and the scherzo from Prokofieff's LOVE OF THREE ORANGES is an effective accompaniment for the witches' sequence in MACBETH. Mood music to accompany motion pictures is now of a remarkably high standard. In many sequences it is essential, yet the audience is often unaware of the fact that music is being played. The legitimate theatre can employ this technique with telling effect, but seldom does because of traditional but no longer significant technical limitations.

The Performer

Nothing is so disconcerting to a performer as the feeling that he is sounding into empty air. In addition, his almost daily use of the telephone has familiarized him with the value of hearing himself. As a result, in a large or non-reverberant hall or studio he tends to increase his vocal or instrumental level, up to the point where sound is reflected to his ears, even though this be above his proper performing level. This effort may lead him into technical errors and overload the PA system if there is one. To provide the assurance and ease necessary for the performer, the sound of the performance must be returned to him by mechanical or electro-acoustic means, at the level he requires. This is later described as the Acoustic Envelope.

Sound as an artist's medium is modified by the ear and the nervous system of the listener. But this is not the only set of limitations imposed upon a sound after it is generated, for what gets to the listener must usually first be affected by the architecture of the theatre and the scenery on the stage.

CHAPTER III

ARCHITECTURE AND SCENERY

THIS BOOK does not set forth the procedure by which an acoustically good theatre is planned. For information on acoustical requirements for theatres the reader is referred to THEATRES AND AUDITORIUMS, 2nd. ed., Expanded 1975, by Burris-Meyer and Cole; and for the processes and procedures for filling these requirements to ACOUSTICS FOR THE ARCHITECT, by Burris-Meyer and Goodfriend. The problem here posed is how to get on the most effective show in the theatre at hand.

The objective of architectural acoustics and of mechanical and electronic sound control is to get the auditory element of the performance to the listeners' positions throughout the house at the same time and with the same characteristics of spectrum and intensity. Moreover, as indicated in Chapter I, sound must appear to come from any place or a moving source or nowhere. The problem of achieving total uniform auditory effect is complex because the sound originally comes from more than one place, except in the case of a single performer. In fact, the sound usually comes to the listener from the stage, but it must also come from the pipe organ, from the orchestra (in the pit), from above the audience, from the back of the house, from the walls, and in a few cases from the floor.

DISTRIBUTION

On its way from the source to the listener's ear, the sound proceeds by many paths. Part of it is reflected from ceiling and walls. Part of it gets to the auditor after it has been reflected back and forth about the house many times. Part of it has been for a trip around the stage, or has been reflected from the scenery or cyclorama. Some has passed through scenic materials. Much of it has been absorbed. The experienced singer, actor, or speaker will often adjust his delivery and sometimes his position on the stage to take advantage of the best acoustical conditions in the house when they are, as they often are, non-uniform.

REFLECTION

A substantial portion of the sound comes to the listener by reflection. In the acoustically well-designed theatre, ceiling and walls will reflect the sound to the audience. Much of the sound from the orchestra in the old Metropolitan Opera House was reflected to the audience from the cove where the proscenium wall meets the ceiling.

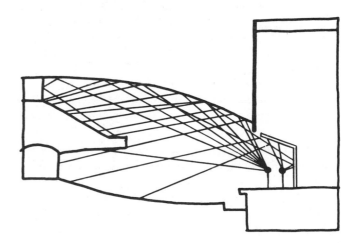

Paths of reflected sound: Section. The upstage source illustrates the function of the concert set.

Non-symmetrical walls, convex balcony fascia, ceilings with reflective panels which slope progressively downward toward the back of the house, are familiar architectural devices to break up multiple reflections, and reinforce the sound in the areas farthest from the stage. The hard-surfaced concert set reflects sound to the audience.

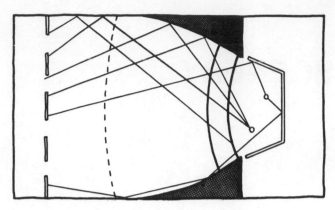

Paths of reflected sound: Plan.

Where the ceiling surface is soft and sound-absorbent, it fails in its primary function—that of distributing sound—and this deficiency must be compensated for by electronic sound-reinforcing equipment.

Where the rear wall is hard and curved, it may focus the sound it reflects on part of the seating area and sometimes the stage, and make speech overlap to the point of unintelligibility. This condition exists in a few theatres to such an extent that rehearsals cannot be held in the empty theatre because the actors cannot understand each other.

Where wall surfaces are parallel and reflective, sound may reflect back and forth between them. This phenomenon, known as flutter, puts the sound *zing* on the end of every word or other sound in the area. One well-known dance studio has a bad flutter between floor and ceiling which annoys performers and distresses the audience.

Where the length of the path of the first reflected wave is more than 75 feet longer than the path of the direct wave, there is an echo, a very annoying feature in some hundreds of seats in a famous motion picture presentation house.

The walls of the stagehouse are generally effective reflecting surfaces. Sound projected into an empty fly loft therefore

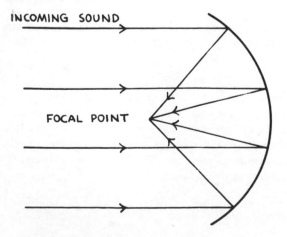

SECTION OF
CONCAVE SURFACE

INCOMING SOUND

FOCAL POINT

has a reverberant pervasive quality which seems large without being loud. This technique was effectively applied to the voice in the Great Boyg scene in PEER GYNT, at the ANTA Playhouse, 1950. (Chapter V, Problem 16.)

All surfaces reflect some frequencies more effectively than others. Usually the differences are at the ends of the spectrum. *Therefore, frequency control of reproduced sound is required to compensate for what is lost in reflection.*

ABSORPTION

All the sound generated in the theatre continues to be reflected about the house and stage until it is absorbed. A negligible amount escapes through openings. All surfaces in the theatre absorb some sound. The softer the material—velour, carpet, draperies, sound-absorbent wall-surfacing materials—the more sound it will absorb. A fly loft full of flown scenery will absorb a lot of sound.

Conversely, plaster, plywood, concrete, brick, metal, all smooth hard-surfaced materials, will reflect sound efficiently and absorb little. A hard concert set helps project the sound from the stage. A velour backdrop may look elegant but is no help to the actor in making himself heard. Padding the back wall of the house keeps the sound from bouncing back to the stage.

Scenic materials reflect sound with an efficiency directly proportional to their stiffness and hardness of surface. A box set will reflect sound better than a plein-air set before a cloth cyclorama. Back-painted flat scenery will reflect more and transmit less sound than scenery painted on one side only. A plaster cyclorama is a very effective reflecting surface, so much so that it must be designed to avoid focusing sound in the audience area. Standing in front of a badly designed hard cyclorama, the actor will be inaudible in some seats and heard in stentorian tones in others. If the cyclorama is tipped back so that it reflects sound to the house ceiling and into the back of the proscenium, it will be acoustically satisfactory and, of course, easier to light than a vertical cyclorama.

People absorb sound and so do seats. In the well-designed theatre each empty seat absorbs as many sabins at the same frequencies as the seat plus a person sitting in it; the total absorption (and therefore the reverberation time) will be unchanged irrespective of the size of the audience. An audience of children will absorb less sound than a matinee audience of women shoppers. Stiff shirt fronts and bare shoulders are reflective as compared to soft shirts and afternoon dresses. This, as has been previously pointed out, makes the traditional first night audience at least acoustically live.

No theatre is or should be as reverberant as a Gothic cathedral, but a scene set in a cathedral, as in FAUST, should sound authentically reverberant, and that's a condition quite different from the garden scene in the same opera. (Chapter V, Problem 19.)

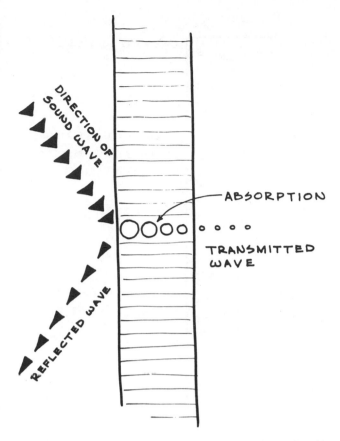

Action of sound encountering a solid surface: Reflection (the angle of incidence equals the angle of reflection), Absorption, and Transmission.

REVERBERATION

Reverberation time has a bearing upon the audibility of the performance (essentially an architectural consideration), on

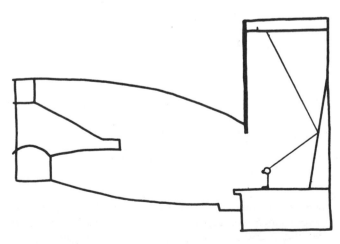

A hard cyclorama tipped back to prevent sound focus in the house. (It is also easy to light.)

the artistic effectiveness of the performer (the showman's concern), and upon the ease and confidence with which the performer approaches his task, as described in Chapter II. Particularly in music, some reverberation is essential to adequate performance. The proof lies in the enthusiastic public acceptance of J. P. Maxfield's reintroduction of liveness into broadcast pickup and recording of music (1947). The subjectively determined reverberation time for types of performance and theatre size is shown in the chart on page 14.

RESONANCE

Akin to reverberation is resonance; the persistence and intensity of the sound at certain discrete frequencies. Of two notes sung at the same intensity, or two harmonics of the same note, one will last longer and sound louder than the other. Every theatre resonates at certain frequencies. One concert singer carried all his songs in three keys, tested the hall before the concert and used the key in which the song was most effectively projected by exploiting the resonant characteristics of the house. But manpower alone will not compensate for acoustical limitations.

Most existing theatres originally built for opera, musical shows, or legitimate productions are moderately live, i.e., they have much hard interior reflecting surface. They are often excessively reverberant with the house empty, and are resonant at one or more frequencies. Motion picture theatres and cabarets are generally not reverberant. Open-air theatres, lacking a ceiling and walls to reflect the sound, are acoustically dead and usually need sound reinforcement and occasionally artificial reverberation. A few exceptionally good theatres have been built within the last decade, some even employ mechanical means: curtains, movable walls and ceilings, which control reverberation time.

Dr. Paul Boner has developed a systematic method for the equalization of sound system frequency response to match the deficiencies of the room or hall. He uses sharply tuned narrow band filters to remove sound energy from the reproduced signal at the frequencies of the room resonances or *ringing* frequencies or modes. This results in a room or hall in which feedback does not occur at the usual levels but is suppressed to an extent that allows, under optimum conditions, 10 or 12 decibels more amplification. For large reverberant coliseums or convention halls, this system is indispensable if a high percent of articulation is to be achieved. The additional amplification is, however, obtained at the price of limiting the loudspeakers to those for which the system has been equalized and limiting the area in which microphones may be used. Under other operating conditions the system again becomes about the same as conventional systems. One effect of room equalization is to remove much of the coloration of the sound that makes one hall distinguishable from another and gives each hall its desirable or undesirable acoustical character.

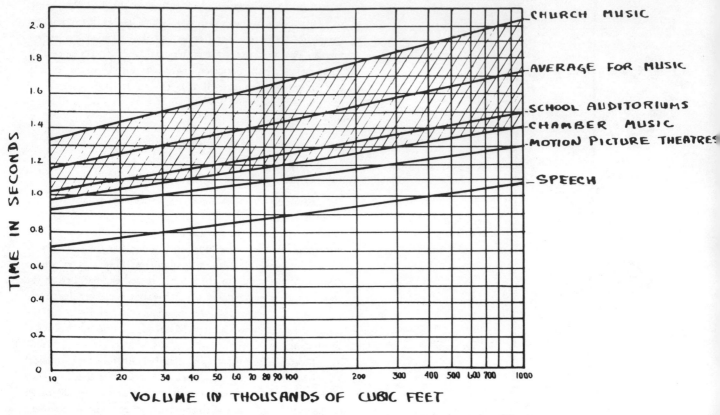

Y-axis: TIME IN SECONDS (0, 0.2, 0.4, 0.6, 0.8, 1.0, 1.2, 1.4, 1.6, 1.8, 2.0)

X-axis: VOLUME IN THOUSANDS OF CUBIC FEET (10, 20, 30, 40, 50, 60, 70, 80, 90, 100, 200, 300, 400, 500, 600, 700, 1000)

CHURCH MUSIC
AVERAGE FOR MUSIC
SCHOOL AUDITORIUMS
CHAMBER MUSIC
MOTION PICTURE THEATRES
SPEECH

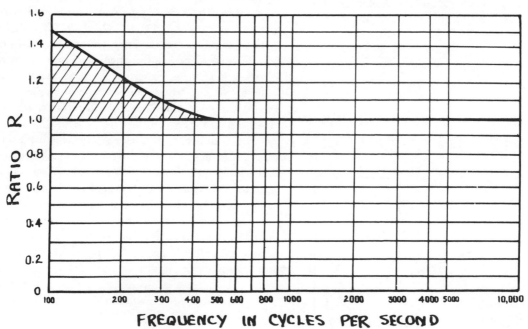

Y-axis: RATIO R (0, 0.2, 0.4, 0.6, 0.8, 1.0, 1.2, 1.4, 1.6)

X-axis: FREQUENCY IN CYCLES PER SECOND (100, 200, 300, 400, 500, 600, 800, 1000, 2000, 3000, 4000, 5000, 10,000)

Optimum reverberation times as set forth in *ACOUSTICAL DE-SIGNING IN ARCHITECTURE*, by Vern O. Knudsen and Cyril M. Harris. The values in the upper figure are all for 1000 cycles. When calculating reverberation for lower frequencies it is nec-essary to modify the equation with a ratio R as shown in the lower chart. For example, $t_f = t_{500} R$. or, in a 100,000 cu. ft. hall the time at 200 Hz = time at 500 Hz $\times$ 1.2 or 1.45 sec.

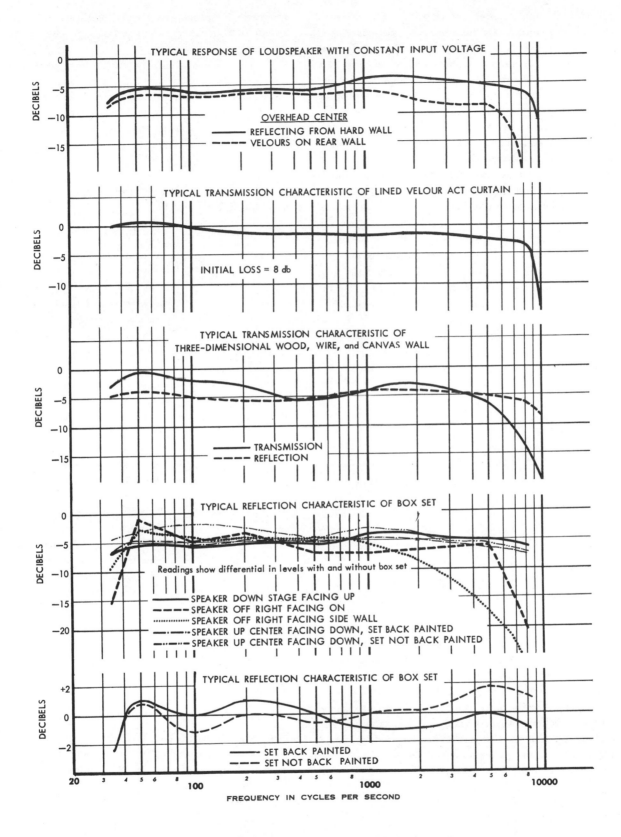

ACOUSTICAL PROPERTIES OF SCENIC MATERIALS

In addition to the system developed by Dr. Boner, a system using one-third octave band filters has been developed for the same purpose. Neither system is really suited to the theatre. Every show requires different arrangements of system components and the almost unreal *clean* voice quality is seldom appropriate for the theatre. In general, not more than five of the Boner type filters remove the worst ring mode frequencies in a theatre sound system. Such equalization may require that microphones be located near the apron center stage and the loudspeakers overhead in the proscenium.

Able architects and acoustical engineers who do not appreciate the scope and subtlety required of sound by playwright and composer continue to build theatres with galling deficiencies. Except in the few—very few—well-designed theatres, the reverberation time changes with the size of the audience. And even the best architectural acoustical design will not provide, without electronic assistance, for varying demands in the same production, as in the previously mentioned non-reverberant garden scene and the highly reverberant scene in the church in FAUST.

So the showman must work with what he has. Some productions, when they move, rehearse in the new house before performing there to discover and compensate as they may for acoustical limitations.

TRANSMISSION

As will be noted in the illustrations, scenic materials transmit some frequencies with relative efficiency while others are attenuated by being absorbed and reflected by the material. *The frequent necessity of concealing loudspeakers behind set pieces, which transmit some frequencies more efficiently than others, illustrates the need for frequency control in the sound system so that compensation may be provided for the attenuated parts of the spectrum.*

Sound projected toward the audience through scenery at high level, or through much scenery, is also modified by the acoustical characteristics of the stage and fly loft. It is, therefore, a good rule to interpose as little material as possible between loudspeaker and audience where precise definition of sound is required. In MADAM, WILL YOU WALK, a hole was cut in the back wall of one set, concealed by a vase of flowers, to allow the direct projection of speech.

Effect sounds on the other hand, such as a passing train or the cavalry in Schnitzler's THE CALL OF LIFE or the carousel music in LILIOM gain the distant and spacious characteristics they require by being projected into the stagehouse and thence transmitted through the set.

NOISE

Unwanted sound is noise. Noise in the theatre masks portions of the show and limits subtlety. The average noise level

in existing metropolitan theatres with audiences present is almost 50 dB in the speech frequencies. A good theatre has less than a 40 dB ambient.

The showman is usually stuck with noise resulting from what the architect planned or didn't plan, but he can make some improvement with draperies, carpets, ground cloth, door seals and the like. The following table is excerpted from an architect's check list and may show the showman where to look for trouble.

AIRBORNE NOISE ORIGINATING OUTSIDE THE HOUSE

Ingress	Method of Exclusion
Doors	Airtight fit. (This is requisite for efficient operation of ventilation system also.) Doors opening on alleys or halls are often less of a problem than if they open on the street.
Windows	Do not belong in a theatre; seal and drape if present.
Ceiling cuts	Exclude sound from loft above the ceiling. Minimize cuts.
Projection booth	Quiet machines; install sound-absorbent walls and ceiling in booth and windows in viewing ports.
Ventilation ducts	1. No metal connection between blower and steel structural members. 2. Ducts large enough not to rattle or whistle when blower operates at full speed (above normal operating speed). 3. Sound absorbent lined ducts.

AIRBORNE NOISE ORIGINATING IN THEATRES

Source	Method of Prevention
Stage wagons, discs (Noise magnified because of reverberant stage floor)	1. Well made ball or roller bearing, rubber tired casters running on level tracks installed over stage floor. 2. Revolving stage on its own support structure. (quieter than disc on stage floor).
Stage elevators	Elevators are quiet unless they are of the screw jack type and run too fast.

Audience (talk, shuffling)	1. Make rear crossover as sound absorbent as possible. (carpet, drappery on reary wall). 2. Lobby doors opposite aisles not used during show. 3. Divide rear crossover from house by a wall—a glass wall for motion picture houses. (This eliminates the rail). 4. Carpet. 5. Silent seats.
Orchestra pit	Rubber feet on chair legs and stands. Carpet on the orchestra pit floor will reduce reflection from the floor and thereby reduce the level of the music.
Shifts	Well built and adequately braced scenery. Well rehearsed shift. *Note:* The noisy shift spoils the entr'acte music.
Snoring	Put on a good show.

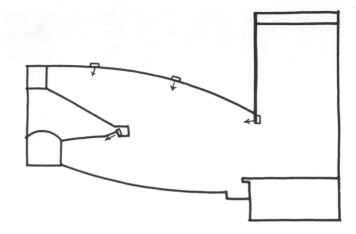

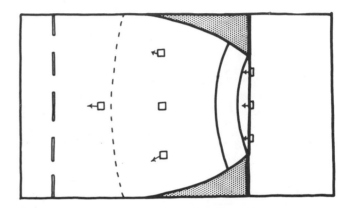

Permanent Installation: Loudspeakers in the ceiling and proscenium for movement and auditory perspective in the house. Proscenium loudspeakers for stereophonic reinforcement also.

STRUCTURE-BORNE NOISE

Source	*Method of Prevention*
Motors, machinery	Vibration isolation mounts.
Switches	Mercury switches

LOUDSPEAKER PLACEMENT

Architecture and scenery may impose limits on loudspeaker placement when electronic sound control or reinforcement is employed. The demands of the performance, the normal behavior of sound unreinforced in the theatre and the characteristics of the ear establish the requirements the loudspeakers must fulfill.

A good rule to remember is "Loudspeakers should be heard but not seen." The purpose of the theatre is to provide illusion. To preserve illusion, loudspeakers must be so placed that the sound will come or seem to come from the logical source. Although the loudspeaker is the actual source, the logical source is the motivating source. The voice of the ghost of Hamlet's father comes from *beneath* the stage and the song of the lark from overhead. All illusion will be lost if these sounds come out of conspicuous cabinets hung from the rail of the balcony box.

Loudspeaker hung from an upstage light bridge in the old Metropolitan Opera House. The sound, reflected from the walls and floor and filtered through scenery, appeared to come from a great distance.

Loudspeakers hung to project through the proscenium opening. Old Metropolitan Opera House. They are completely masked by the valance.

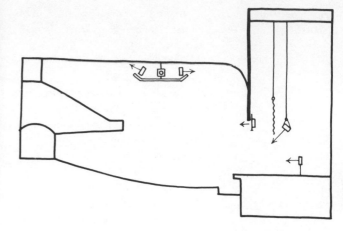

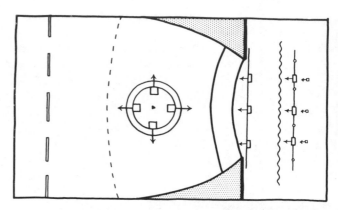

Temporary loudspeaker mounting positions: Four loudspeakers in the chandelier reflecting from ceiling and walls, three in a false proscenium, others hung behind a masking border and set on stands upstage for dubbing.

The installations here illustrated are designed to take care of any requirement in that by the use of one or the sequential or simultaneous use of many loudspeakers, the sound may be made to come from any source or no source or a moving source.

When the installation is made for a particular show with limited requirements, a less elaborate setup will usually do. But aside from special effects such as the talking bottle in HAPPY BIRTHDAY, or the subsonic drum in THE EMPEROR JONES, (Stevens Theatre, 1941) which used the house floor as a loudspeaker element, no permanent loudspeaker locations are needed in addition to those illustrated.

When there is no chandelier and there are no ceiling loudspeakers, loudspeakers mounted anywhere so that they will reflect sound from the ceiling without direct sound reaching the audience, will serve the purpose of ceiling loudspeakers. In Sidney Howard's MADAM, WILL YOU WALK, loudspeakers placed in the upper boxes directed toward the ceiling caused the music of the celestial orchestra to come to the audience by reflection from the ceiling; and, in view of the ear's inability to judge altitude, the music was present everywhere, but came from nowhere, from no identifiable source.

Caution: The unforgivable, and still-too-common, sin is to mount loudspeakers on either side of the proscenium, pointed directly at the audience, for simple reinforcement. This system makes the audience everywhere, except on the center line, hear both loudspeakers one after the other, with a result that all illusion of reality is destroyed and in some locations speech becomes unintelligible and music, noise.

CHAPTER IV

SOURCES AND PICKUP

SOUND has to come from somewhere. Traditionally the character of the source dictated its position with respect to the audience. The opera aria was sung from down center. The string bass were placed behind the other instruments in the orchestra. While some of these conventions conform to other theatrical requirements, some do not.

Electronic control makes it possible to locate the source where it is dramatically most effective and can give it the desired character.

VOICE

The human voice is the most important sound source in the theatre. The voice has a dynamic range from the threshold of audibility to more than 90 dB (opera singers at 3 feet) and substantially more than that for hog callers. A basso can sing notes below 90 Hz and a soprano may reach approximately 1200 Hz for the fundamental tone. The rich voice will have measurable harmonics to 16,000 Hz or higher. The relative intensity of harmonics varies between voices and from note to note in the same voice, and may be modified during the singing of a single note. In a vibrato, there is a change of fundamental usually less than a semitone.

The identity of words is established by the consonants in which high frequencies predominate. The harmonic structure of the voice establishes its identity and can be varied within the individual voice to convey a wide gamut of emotion.

When the voice in speech or song is distorted by mechanical or electronic means, it loses reality. Distortion of speech by public address systems is too often tolerated, but it has no place in the theatre except where it is specifically required by the play. (Chapter V, Problems 8 and 12.) Because of its complexity and flexibility, the human voice requires greater fidelity of sound control apparatus than does any other source. It is also, and by the same token, susceptible of the most subtle and effective use in the theatre.

MUSICAL INSTRUMENTS, ORCHESTRAS

Conventional musical instruments constitute the second most important sound source. The balanced orchestra capable of playing most standard orchestral scores consists of approximately 35 instruments as a minimum. This number exceeds the number of different instruments to be sure, but multiple instruments, especially in the strings, are required for intensity and balance and for the rich harmonic structure which comes from the simultaneous playing of the same note by a number of instruments. The orchestra for grand opera in houses seating 3500 to 5000 and for motion picture presentation in houses of similar size has about 75 pieces—occasionally being augmented to about 100 or more, especially for open-air opera. These sizes are dictated largely by the need for intensity enough to fill the large house. The special requirements of Wagnerian opera caused Wagner to load up his pit with bass viols. This bass deficiency, or for that matter any demand requiring special emphasis or intensity can be met by selective amplification (Chapter V, Problem 6.)

Small orchestras have about eight instruments; specialty orchestras may have any number, depending upon the special instrumentation involved.

The pit orchestra for musical shows conventionally numbers about 26. However, there is no rule. Some shows open with a large orchestra which is cut down after the first few weeks. Costs and union contracts often have more to do with the size of the orchestra than does the music.

Contract houses which guarantee full season employment to a minimum number of musicians (6 to 10) must use this number or more on every show. This situation accounts for the very unimaginative and trite *entr'acte* music found in some large houses when non-musical shows are playing. Any trouper remembers houses on the road in which a number of chairs in the pit were occupied by people who held instruments but could not play them. The musicians union has often been quite arbitrary in placing demands upon houses and declaring them unfair and pulling off the other unions if its demands for employment were not met irrespective of whether or not musical shows were presented.

In a musical presented in 1931 in the Stevens Theatre the set was built out over the pit. The orchestra was located in a studio next to the theatre and the entire musical score piped in. By taking the orchestra out of the pit it was possible to give a very small orchestra the necessary dynamics, and a blending which would have been impossible in the pit. The added advantage of removing the orchestra as a visual distraction was noted, although it should be mentioned here that the visual presence of an orchestra often contributes to the total effect especially in presentation shows. A remote orchestra was employed in New York two seasons later by Earl Carroll but, because the reproducing equipment was of inferior quality and poorly handled, the attempt was not a success and the orchestra was moved to a box. However, these deficiencies have been overcome in subsequent productions: Clifford Odets' NIGHT MUSIC; Anita Loos' HAPPY BIRTHDAY, and THE ETERNAL ROAD, to mention a few.

Small backstage orchestras have been, and are, necessary in some productions: Max Gordon's production of PRIDE AND PREJUDICE and BALLO IN MASCHERA at the Metropolitan.

An offstage orchestra onstage is hard to handle. There isn't enough light. The musicians' chairs and stands are in the way of the shifts. The music is filtered through the set and loses presence, and the direction is restricted. It is therefore well to exert some electronic control over music from the orchestra no matter where it is located. If it does not appear in the pit, it is best located in an acoustically appropriate studio away from the stage.

EFFECTS

Effects include all sounds required by the production other than speech, song, or instrumental music. They are potentially very important to the production in that they create, reinforce, or counterpoint the atmosphere or mood; reveal character; or contribute to the advancement of the plot. In a sense they fulfill the function of music as illustrated by the fact that musical figures can often be substituted for effects and serve as background music. In conformity with the principle that music is a way of handling sound, effects treated according to the principles of musical composition can achieve an emotional response as does conventional music. (Chapter I, CYRANO, recording score; Chapter X, PROMETHEUS, operating script.) Sound effects need not be faithful reproductions of the sounds concerned. It will often suffice if only some salient significant element of a sound is reproduced. As in the case of dialect speech, where the actor employs enunciation designed for the best projection but the cadence of the dialect, his reading of the lines will often be accepted as dialect. Some effects have significance on the basis of their sheer psycho-physical impact, as the bombing in IDIOTS DELIGHT, and the drum in THE EMPEROR JONES.

Orchestra, including organ and piano, playing in a reverberant dressing room in NIGHT MUSIC. Electronic control provided flexibility impossible for music played from the orchestra pit.

PROP SOUND SOURCES

Traditionally, sound effect devices belong in the property department. The prop shop builds them, the property man maintains, handles, and operates them. Most of them are theatrically obsolete because of the ready availability of recordings of almost any conceivable sound. Radio developed an elaborate array of sound effect devices which, however, were designed to satisfy the restricted requirements of that medium. These have diminishing value as the stock libraries of recorded effects increase and improve and since it is so easy to make recordings on tape of any special effect that is needed. Although recordings do better than prop or radio effects for most situations, there are some effects which place such heavy demands on the electronic reproducing systems that it is better to use the prop device. Also some prop devices are so simple, cheap, and easy to cue that it is advantageous to use them if there is no other use for electronic sound reproducing equipment in the production. When special tapes are made for the show, it is sometimes simplest to create the effects with mechanical devices and record them. Some companies which make stage lighting instruments also make mechanical sound apparatus. A table of mechanical sound effect devices follows.

Caution: Because of the flexibility possible with electronic sources and equipment, there is a tendency to depend on such gear when *conventional mechanical devices would be adequate or better*. Very few sound reproducing systems are adequate to reproduce faithfully the crash of glass. None can reproduce a shot from a large calibre weapon or an explosion near at hand since the amount of power put into the air by an explosion is so much greater than that of which the electronic sound reproducing system is capable. Therefore, explosive effects which must be immediate or close must be the real thing.

MECHANICAL SOUND EFFECTS

Effect	Apparatus	Technique of Operation	Comment
animal noises	made vocally by a specialist in the craft; wind instruments sometimes used for frogs, cattle, poultry; special whistles for bird calls		
	for sound of bull, dog, lion, etc., a bull roarer; a can, piece of sheet metal, wood, fiber, or drumhead, to which is attached a resined string or thong; materials vary with sound required	draw thong taut; rub with resined cloth	
artillery	*see* thunder		
bells	bells, pipe chimes, lengths of pipe, automobile brake drums, or any suitably pitched piece of metal hung free in a frame	strike	It is best to use the real article if single notes are to be struck on cue.
bombs	1. where fire regulations permit: smokeless powder bombs made up in heavy cardboard, plus squibs, batteries, wire, metal barrel	set squib in bomb, wire to current source; place bomb in barrel; to fire, close circuit. *Caution:* disconnect both wires from current source and firing switch before wiring squib; one man only does all wiring	Where the explosions are distant, reproduction through electronic amplifying systems is adequate. For nearby explosions, which exceed output of the electronic system, No. 2 and No. 3 are recommended.
	2. metal barrel, 12-gauge double-barreled shotgun, blank shells	fire shotgun into barrel; both barrels may be fired simultaneously if necessary. *Caution:* piece is loaded just before firing by man who fires; shells are kept in his, and only his, possession	
	3. heavy padded weight	drop on reverberant floor	
chimes	*see* bells		
crashes, wood	a spiked drum mounted in a frame; slats are fastened in one end of frame and rest snugly against drum at loose end	rotate drum with crank	More flexible and effective results may be achieved by breaking splint fruit baskets before the microphone.
	slapstick and lattice (thunder board)	strike a number of boards with one stroke of the stick	
	laths set up in a slotted plank like an open picket fence	break laths with hammer	
door slam	door in frame	fairly obvious	Still effective when fitted with proper hardware.
	wooden chest	slam lid	
	3′ piece of 1″ × 3″	place end on floor, press downward on that end with foot; hold other end away from floor; release	
elevated	*see* train of cars		
explosions	*see* bombs		

Effect	Apparatus	Technique of Operation	Comment
fire	crumbled piece of cellophane held in hand; sound system	manipulated near microphone to produce crackling sound	
gas, escaping	compressed air	valve	
	tacks and small metal chute	pour tacks down chute	
glass crash	box of broken glass	drop the box. *Caution:* when glass is broken onstage, prop men wear gloves and tight-fitting goggles; a cloth is laid to catch broken glass where practical	This method is still effective; especially for microphone pickup.
hail	rain drum (*see* rain)	revolve rapidly	
hoofbeats, cavalry	coconut shells	strike together or against a flat surface in cadence; padded surface used to simulate footfalls on earth; various materials give different pitches	This system is very effective when no electronic amplifying system is available. When a microphone is available, this effect is better simulated by striking the chest with the palms of the hands according to a predetermined cadence. Various pitches result from either shirt, waistcoat, or jacket.
horn	*see* whistle		
industrial noises	chain run through blocks, ratchets, riveting machines, electric hammer, etc.	operate in conventional manner; pound pipes, floor, pinrail, etc.	
locomotive	snare drum, wire brushes	beat or rub the side, rim, or head of the drum with the brushes	
	sandpaper mounted on blocks	rub two pieces together	
	trombone	remove mouthpiece; blow in cadence	
	sheet metal, $2' \times 2'$; wire brushes	beat sheet with the brushes	
	shot in dishpan covered by another pan	shake	
machine gun	*see* crashes, wood (1)		
marching feet	a square frame, $2' \times 2'$-$4'$ within which is stretched a string net of $1\,\frac{1}{2}''$ mesh; a $\frac{1}{2}''$-$1''$ dowel stick, $4''$-$6''$ long, is hung from each string intersection	raise and lower frame in cadence, so dowel ends strike a surface of whatever reverberant characteristics are desired	
	bass drum or kettledrum	strike in cadence with a number of padded drumsticks	
metal crash	a metal barrel, can, or tub full of scrap hardware	drop can or tub, or pour scrap from one container to another	This method is still effective; especially for microphone pickup.
	junk chute; a rough metal chute, 60° to horizontal, $10'$-$30'$ long	pour junk metal down chute	
motorboat	*see* automobile		
music	offstage musicians or orchestra		
rain	shallow metal plate containing handful of dried peas or rice	oscillate plate	
	perforated pipe over trough equipped with drain	run water through pipe	Too great realism in reproducing sounds of rain may result in considerable discomfort to the audience.

Effect	Apparatus	Technique of Operation	Comment
	rain drum: a barrel or drum mounted on a frame on bearings, os it can revolve on its long axis; longitudinal slats set 2''-6'' apart on inner surface; dried beans, peas, or rice placed in barrel	revolve barrel	
	rain chute: dried beans in bag which tapers to 1'' opening hung over hopper; hopper opens into chute 4'-15' long and 6''-12'' square; top and bottom of chute are of canvas; sides, of wood; bottom canvas crossed by slats placed inside, 4''-10'' apart; tub at bottom of chute to catch beans; chute 45°-60° to horizontal	hold small end of bag in hand; release grasp to allow beans to run into hopper	
shots	pistols, shotguns; some stage weapons are constructed to fire blank ammunition only	*see* caution under "artillery"	
	leather-covered chair cushion, suitcase, or stretched hide; switches	beat cushion, suitcase, or hide with switches	This is an excellent system for simulating distant and even nearby shots.
sirens	the genuine articles when possible	operate by hand power or electrically. *Caution:* make certain correct current is used	Excellent records available.
steam, escaping	*see* gas, escaping		
subway	*see* train of cars		
surf	*see* thunder drum and barrel; rain		
	teeter trays: similar to goldwashing cradles; dried beans or peas placed in tray	rock floor or tray through 100°	
	rain drum (*see* rain)	rock slowly	
thunder	16- to 24-gauge galvanized sheet metal, 30''-36'' × 6'-14', battened top and bottom hung offstage	shake bottom batten, beat sheet with mallet or hammer; pitch varies with gauge, area, and violence of shaking	This is still an effective instrument. It is far superior to low-power electronic reproducers to simulate distant thunder. It is inferior to higher power (500 watts or over) electronic systems for simulating nearby thunder.
	sheet profile board, hung offstage	shake or beat like sheet metal above	
	thunder drum: hide stretched on rigid wooden frame, about 3' × 4', with resonant chamber underneath	beat with padded mallet (must be heated before using; an electric light bulb will suffice)	
	drum-ended resonating barrel; pitch varies with diameter and length	beat with padded mallet; pitch varies with distance of blow from center of drum; intensity varies with power of blow	
	rumble wagon: a small wagon with hexagonal wheels, heavily weighted	roll on reverberant floor	
	thunder board: a number of boards made up like a Venetian blind, hung offstage on one line	release the line	
train of cars	four metal-tired casters mounted on the ends of a 3-foot 2'' × 4'' X-frame; center of X-frame pivoted above a box on which is mounted a circular metal track, 5/16'' thick, split at two places, 110° apart; casters run on the track	rotate X-frame; box may be modified to give different reverberation characteristics of subway, surface car, or elevated	

Effect	*Apparatus*	*Technique of Operation*	*Comment*
underbrush	burlap sack filled 2/3's full of white flake glue and securely sewed or tied shut	walk on bag	This method is still effective when amplified. In addition, actual underbrush may be used.
	open tray of flake glue	walk on the glue	
whistle	the genuine article when possible; or organ pipes	blow by lung power, bellows, mechanical or electrical blowers, or compressed air	Excellent records available.
wind	slatted drum mounted on bearings; sheet of cloth fastened to mounting frame, passing over drum, and battened at free end; pitch varies with texture of cloth; canvas generally used	rotate drum toward free end of cloth; pull canvas taut; pitch and intensity vary with speed and canvas tension	
	strips of bamboo or umbrella ribs fastened to shaft of variable-speed electric motor	run motor; speed governs pitch	
	blower	run motor	

Three time-honored sound effect devices. Background: a rumble cart produces varying sounds as its cargo is changed. Left foreground: subway train, trolley cars, or railway cars according to the loading on the revolve and the speed of rotation. Right foreground: a bull roarer which produces various animal sounds as operator varies the tension in the cord with one hand and varies the way he strokes the cord with a rosin-coated glove on the other hand. He stands on the base to which the boiler is fastened.

RECORDS

Disc records of most sounds used in the theatre are available from a number of sources. Many are made from motion picture sound tracks and, if reproduced with good enough equipment, will provide a signal which is quite acceptable under demanding circumstances. The variety is wide. When the cry of the kookaburra bird was required for Bemelmans' NOW I LAY ME DOWN TO SLEEP, it was found almost immediately in a stock recording of tropical bird noises.

But the disc record has no place in the performance except as a practical prop used onstage. Even then, it is safer to play the number over the sound system from a tape, with the loudspeaker in or upstage of the record player and fake the operation of the record player onstage.

Disc recordings have two limitations; they deteriorate rapidly in use, and they are extremely difficult to cue. The stage is a dusty place. Despite precautions, dust gets in the grooves of the disc and makes it noisy. For Piscator's production of KING LEAR special discs were made for the show and a new one had to be used at each performance.

The legitimate production plays many times, the pace of each performance varying with the audience response. This makes time cueing of disc records impossible and fast cueing impractical. In the Norman Bel Geddes production of HAMLET in which a special recorded score was used, it proved impossible to cue a recorded drum roll to Hamlet's appearance at Ophelia's funeral so that an actual kettle drum had to be brought in.

The two limitations cited are easily overcome by making up the show on tape which can be marked with visual cues so

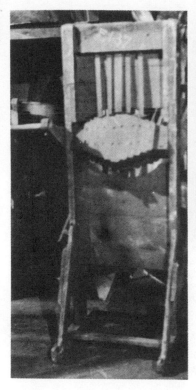

PROP EFFECTS: Left, wood crash; above, thunder drum, front and rear.

that great cueing precision is possible. Because reproduction from tape is magnetic rather than mechanical, the quality of the record does not deteriorate with use. Tape has the additional advantages of making it possible to: (a), arrange and keep the show in sequence and avoid the possibility of running sounds out of order: (b), employ on single tape material dubbed from records of different speeds or recorded live; (c), edit, cut, and modify and re-record sounds as they may be developed during the preparation of the show; and (d), cue accurately despite variations in running time of the scene. So the disc record is used to make up the show tape. To use it in performance is to invite trouble.

Electronic Music

Sounds can be composed on photographic sound tracks and on magnetic media without ever being mechanically produced and recorded. Modern music thus produced has developed more critical controversy than paying customers. Though a most flexible technique, this procedure has not yet superseded any conventional method of producing or using sound in the theatre.

ELECTRONIC INSTRUMENTS

There are many occasions where sound (and this includes music) must pace the show. Here magnetic records will not do because their pace cannot vary with audience response. Elec-

tronic instruments (fingerboard, keyboard, string tympani) used as sound sources playing through the electronic sound control system can do this job. Moreover, because of their unique ability to imitate almost any sound they may be used to make tape records for the show when records can be used.

Just as electronic instruments can make almost any sound the human imagination can conjure up, the number of instruments which can be used for the wide variety of theatrical requirements is also practically limitless. Listed here are only the most useful instruments of each type.

SYNTHESIZERS

Almost any sound which can be imagined, and probably many which can't, are producible by highly sophisticated synthesizers, darlings of some composers of modern music. The current instruments, no larger than the upright piano, can feed directly into the theatre sound system to be used as part of an orchestra or the whole orchestra; or they can be used to make show tapes of any kind of associative or non-associative sound.

Vocoder

The Vocoder was developed by the Bell Telephone Laboratories as an instrument to be used to study speech. By it, sounds are analyzed and then synthesized. By modifying the synthesis process, it can remake almost any sound to satisfy a

The Moog Synthesizer MK III

theatrical requirement and to blend and combine a number of sounds. The Vocoder was used to make the synthesized voice of an ass speak intelligible speech for A MIDSUMMER NIGHT'S DREAM, to permit Prospero to speak with the voice of wind and thunder in THE TEMPEST, and to give the witches in MACBETH unhuman but credible and appropriate voices. The cost of making records on the Vocoder is high and the technique of using it is complex. These features militate against its use in the theatre.

Sonovox

Many of the theatrical jobs done with the Vocoder can be approximated if not precisely duplicated at much smaller expense with the Sonovox, a device which substitutes the output of a sound system (the vibration of a special loud-speaker unit) for the human larynx. Any sound having the requisite frequency range can thereby be made the material of speech. The bell may speak and so may a police siren or a group of musical instruments.

Artificial Larynx

The Firestone artificial larynx differs only from the Sonovox in that the sound is introduced into the mouth by a vibrated air column rather than the vibration of throat tissues.

The artificial larynx therefore is capable of reproducing higher frequencies than the Sonovox and more complex harmonic structures. With the artificial larynx one person may sing duets, quartets, or choruses, and may speak or sing in the frequency range above or below that which is possible with the normal human voice.

Novachord

The Novachord is perhaps the most universally useful theatrical sound source. It can be employed as a musical instrument and to create stylized or in some cases even realistic effects. Kurt Weill employed it extensively in the productions for which he composed or planned the music. In Elmer Rice's TWO ON AN ISLAND it worked both as a musical instrument and as an effect machine. One of its best uses is illustrated in the Walter Teschan score for PROMETHEUS.

Organs

Electronic organs have the advantage of portability. They can be hooked into the sound systems so sound is distributed to any place which is theatrically requisite and they are not limited, as in the case of the Metropolitan Opera House, to having the organ music come from one place irrespective of the requirements of the scene. Numerous electronic organs are

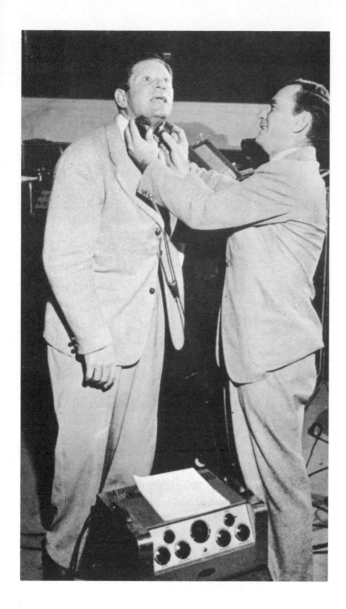

SONOVOX. Sequences requiring this instrument will be recorded and the record used in performance, rather than using the device itself. Gilbert Wright, the inventor, demonstrates to Bob Burns. (*Gene Lester photo*)

The Hammond NOVACHORD

quite satisfactory as musical instruments and the pipe organ, for which they are substitutes, is an instrument of such flexibility and power as to have a great variety of important theatrical uses.

EFFECT MACHINES

Effect machines can be made to synthesize many sounds. Only three of the most useful are listed here: the Novachord, mentioned previously, the thunder screen, and the musical saw. The thunder screen will reproduce any of the crashes except glass. It consists of metal screen stretched on a wood frame with a phonograph pickup element attached to the center of the screen so that screen vibrations actuate the pickup. It can be rubbed, struck, or scratched to reproduce sounds of rolling distant thunder, far away artillery, or machine guns. Devices used with it are brush for striking, flexible pin for scratching. The musical saw used with a microphone makes shrieks or twangs and is in general the electronic equivalent of the bull roarer.

Special devices consisting principally of resistors, capacitors, filters, the Theremin, and ribbon microphones in which the ribbon may be agitated by scraping or blowing, have all been used in the theatre with considerable success though they are capable of producing few effects not possible with the standard devices here enumerated.

General arrangement of Artificial Larynx as used in speaking and singing. Sequences requiring this device should be recorded.

Thunder Screen. The effect here shown is produced by striking the screen with a soft brush and manipulating the channel level control.

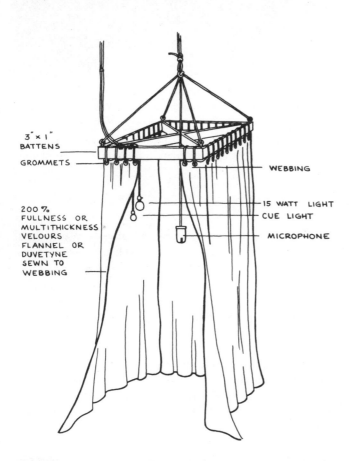

3" × 1" BATTENS

GROMMETS

WEBBING

200 % FULLNESS OR MULTITHICKNESS VELOURS FLANNEL OR DUVETYNE SEWN TO WEBBING

15 WATT LIGHT CUE LIGHT

MICROPHONE

The Microphone Tent reduces backstage noise pickup. It may contain a cue light and a pilot light showing when the microphone is live as well as the hanging microphone. Rigged on a single spot line, it can be taken out when not working.

NOVELTY

The theatre thrives on novelty, and the unfettered imagination of the showman will always demand something which is not at hand. It is reported that Toscanini insisted on using a drum for Verdi's REQUIEM which was so big that it required partial dismantling of the elevator to get it to the broadcasting studio in Radio City. Of course, the radio audience could not hear it but Toscanini could. It is reported that even a bigger drum is used by the Imperial Gagaku Orchestra in Tokyo. The instrumentalist has to use a ladder while beating it and its pitch is so low that it is felt rather than heard. To achieve a subsonic effect in THE EMPEROR JONES, the whole floor of the theatre was vibrated as the diaphragm of a loud-speaker. Gilbert Miller used a tremendous organ pipe to produce a sound bridge for the transition between the centuries in BERKELEY SQUARE but dropped it from the production for fear that it would constitute a harmful distraction.

PICKUP POSITIONS

One of the principal uses of electronic sound control equipment is the freeing of sound from the directional limitations imposed by the location of the source. Pickup by microphone may be made from the stage, backstage, pit, front house, trap room, prop room, dressing room, sound studio, projection booth, or sound control room.

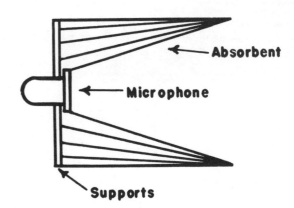

Absorbent

Microphone

Supports

Section of Microphone Enclosure made of multiple thicknesses of flannel or duvetyn.

STAGE

Conventional stage pickup involves footlight microphones and microphones concealed behind the teaser hung from the bridge or first pipe. The hung microphone has the advantage of not picking up floor rumble but has markedly reduced efficiency if not rendered entirely useless when the performer works on the apron. Props are used to conceal stage microphones, a standard practice used by Radio City Music Hall. Offstage pickup is easier than onstage. Floor stands, the simplest devices, are to be avoided wherever possible because they are subject to damage, especially in the dark, and precise distance and orientation with respect to the sound source are difficult to maintain. A hung microphone is much to be preferred.

Wireless microphones the size of a dime may be worn by performers. They use a small electronics package readily concealed on the actor and the cord used to hold them in place serves as the antenna. These microphones are built to operate on frequencies shared with business services except for those used in the television and film industries that are assigned special broadcast service frequencies. Thus it is not unusual to find taxi or repair truck signal coming in on the receiver of nightclub wireless microphones. Careful planning and frequency selection along with the use of special receiving antennas can eliminate the problem.

The widely advertised high fidelity wireless microphones for home use are designed to operate over very short distances and are subject to interference. A major problem of wireless or lavalier microphones worn by the actor is that the pickup characteristic is never as good as that of a microphone in front of the actor. Also the microphone worn on the person can pick up undesired sounds including that of the clothing.

Backstage pickup occurs usually in the case of voice dubbing or when the source of the sound is not to be seen as, for example, the voice of Mephisto in the church scene in FAUST, or the voice of Agamemnon speaking from the mouth of Cassandra (onstage) in Robinson Jeffers' TOWER BEYOND TRAGEDY, or the voice used for the ghost in HAMLET when the ghost is a translucent ectoplasmic figure. Where a single voice source is used, the microphone can be hung in an absorbent (velour, duvetyn, or flannel) tent and flown together with the tent when not in use. The tent can have an open side facing the stage so that the actor can watch for and hear his cues. When the microphone tent is not feasible, an absorbent enclosure constructed so as to permit only the direct sound to reach it can be used at any convenient location backstage. (This enclosure is not to be confused with or replaced by a "directional" cardioid, or shotgun microphone whose purpose is different.) Such an enclosure will exclude all sound except that which comes directly into the open end. Therefore, if it is so hung that there is a flat or screen behind the actor, it is almost as quiet as a microphone tent. Choruses and orchestras picked up backstage as in BALLO or ORFEO produce a sufficiently high sound level so that no special protection against ambient backstage noise need be provided unless a shift is in progress at the time the microphone is open.

Pit. The technique of pickup from orchestra pit is pretty well understood. The larger the orchestra the greater is the flexibility in the location of microphones. Small orchestras require more reinforcement for some instruments than for others. In the case of pit pickup, as for onstage pickup, the directional microphone is usually the most useful since it can respond to the signal from the source toward which it is directed

with much greater efficiency than to other sources in the vicinity. The greater the congestion of instruments in the pit, the more difficult the pickup and the more hazardous because the distance between pickup and microphone may vary from performance to performance or the microphone may be reoriented by moving it while people are entering the pit or leaving it.

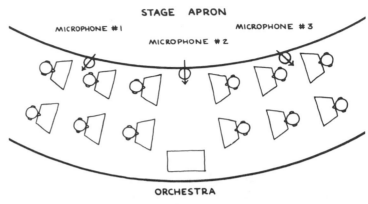

PIT STEREOPHONIC PICKUP

Front House. When it is necessary to reinforce sound using loudspeakers located in the under-balcony ceiling, the pickup from the stage is often impractical. Sound from the stage to the listener's location travels directly in air some 75 feet or more farther than the sound which makes the trip via microphone and loudspeaker. The reproduced sound therefore arrives first and the time difference causes a reduction in intelligibility. In order to avoid substantial time difference between the original and the reproduced sound, it is often necessary to make the pickup from the balcony face. In this case, the signal is, of course, considerably attenuated by the time it reaches the microphone,

Line microphone

and a highly directional microphone may be needed for satisfactory pickup. Front-house pickup of the audience sound may be used to beef up applause. If applause is picked up and played back to the audience, the audience thinks it is applauding louder than it is and so increases its efforts. This technique can sometimes get as many as five curtain calls more than the same show with the same kind of audience and no reinforcement. In such pickup a nondirectional microphone should be hung from the ceiling in an area not covered by a loudspeaker.

Trap Room, Rooms near the Stage, Studio. The offstage pickup locations in a theatre are often small, noisy, and reverberant. Dressing rooms are difficult to use unless the reverberation is reduced by wall hangings, the internal noise limited by carpet, and only a few people or instruments are required for the source. The prop room which was used for offstage choruses at the old Metropolitan needed no special treatment because it was high, contained considerable absorption, and had a large enough floor area to accommodate the chorus comfortably. On many occasions it is necessary to use the trap room for pickup. This is difficult because the stage floor is usually very noisy. A makeshift studio may be improvised by putting a carpet on the trap room floor, curtaining all four sides with velour or such other absorbent material as may be available and making a ceiling of sound absorbent material attached to the underside of the stage floor beams. This is sometimes difficult in view of the necessity of staying clear of the sprinkler pipes and heads. Small

orchestras used in such improvised studios have been quite satisfactory. In Anita Loos' HAPPY BIRTHDAY there were an orchestra, a Hammond organ, and a soloist. While the performance was completely satisfactory and consistent, extraordinary care had to be exercised all the time to maintain the orientation of microphones hung from the sprinkler pipes and the position of the instrumentalists. Where the theatre contains a broadcasting studio, of course, problems just alluded to do not occur.

BALANCE

Where performers can hear each other it often happens that each tries to balance the total performance by adjusting his level to what seems right to him. However, balance must finally be controlled by the conductor or technician who hears it as it goes into the house. To facilitate balance it is sometimes necessary to isolate performers from each other by screens which permit them to hear each other well enough to get the cues but not enough to tempt them to balance the performance. This technique is much used in recording. When the Acoustic Envelope is employed, it acts as an automatic volume control on the singers. This is especially noticeable and most gratifying when one singer has a big voice and another a tiny one.

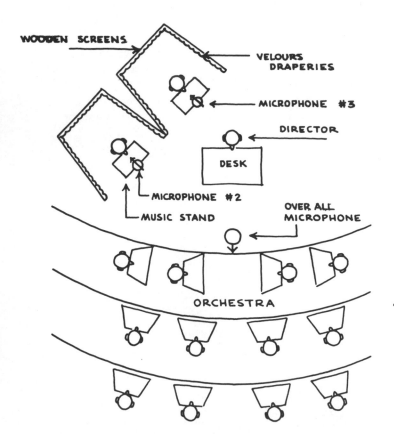

Isolation Screens. The lectern establishes the position of the performer with relation to the hanging microphone.

RECORDING SET UP

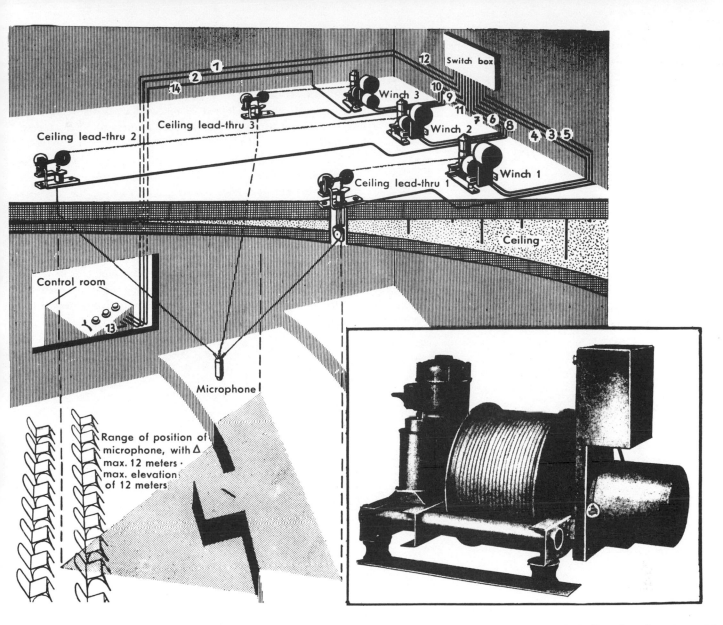

Three-dimensional microphone windlass assembly showing range of position. Inset: Remotely controlled windlass for microphone trim.

MICROPHONE TECHNIQUE

Few microphone-amplifier systems are free from distortion at distances less than a foot from the sound source. Since intensity drops off with distance in accordance with the inverse-square law, it is desirable to have the microphone as near to the sound source as possible without distortion. In theatre reinforcement it is seldom possible to have stage pickup at distances less than eight feet and most pickup has to occur at distances greater than that. The closer the microphone to the sound source the higher the signal is from that source as opposed to random noise or other simultaneous sound sources. By the same token, the farther the microphone is from the sound source the more complete the blending of sound from all simultaneous sources within the theatre. The relative optima for definition,

blending, and liveness have been the subject of much study for purposes of recording and broadcasting pickup. The marked improvement in music—both broadcast and recorded—which began in the 1940s was in large measure due to J. P. Maxfield's mathematical rationalization of the requirements for definition, blending, and liveness, as previously cited.

DISTORTION

An example of the deliberate use of distortion occurred in the synthesizing of the voice of the ghost in HAMLET. The spectrum here illustrated was acceptable as coming from the ectoplasmic translucent figure. In addition to judicious filter-

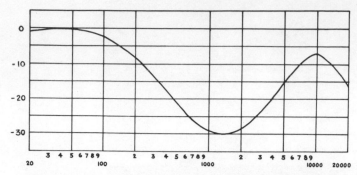

Frequency response of a system required for the voice of the ghost in HAMLET. To achieve the desired amplitude, two frequency-discrimination networks must be used in series, or the actor must work very close to a ribbon microphone without close-talk equalization. This curve does not represent the response the audience hears, of course, since the final signal will be modified by the microphone characteristics, the voice of the actor, and the acoustics of the house.

ing, the effect required the use of a velocity (ribbon) microphone as a pressure instrument by working too close to the ribbon. It is interesting to note that this phenomenon was shortly thereafter adopted in somewhat emasculated form for radio broadcasting and was for a long time part of the standard radio bag of tricks.

Distortion as such now seems to be accepted as a vaudeville or nightclub idiom. The vaudevillian of the pre-electronic era learned to project. He also learned the dramatic value of various forms of vocal distortion, the shout, the howl, and the gravelly enunciation. The present-day performer, who seldom has his father's abilities or training, undertakes to achieve similar end results through the distortions introduced by working too close to the microphone, or in an area where its pickup is not uniformly efficient. No electronic magic can compensate for the shortcomings of the performer, or materially mitigate the rigors of the discipline prerequisite to virtuosity.

CHAPTER V

CONTROL TECHNIQUES

THIS CHAPTER tells what has to be done to the sound to fulfill the theatrical requirement. When the necessary control techniques are established, the systems, equipment, and operating practices treated in the next three chapters may be derived therefrom.

AUDIBILITY

Just as the first function of light in the theatre is to provide visibility, the first requisite of sound is that the audience shall hear the show. The words must not only be heard, they must be understood. The various instruments in the orchestra must have and preserve the balance called for by composer and conductor. Most of these problems are susceptible of solution by mechanical means, by standard architectural acoustical methods, if the house is small enough. However, in houses of over 1000 capacity, there are many acoustical problems which cannot be solved by mechanical means alone. Electronic means must be relied upon to compensate for acoustical shortcomings. Moreover the differing acoustical requirements of varying types of presentation, as lecture or opera, can be met by changing the sound level, the reverberation time, and the spectrum of reflected sound, as well as providing even sound distribution. A system which can accomplish these things increases the flexibility of production even in a small house.

PROBLEM 1. To achieve understandable speech or a satisfactory level for music in a large house (3500 plus).

Discussion: When the sound level is raised, the frequency spectrum is often changed due to the absorption of high frequencies in air and the absorption characteristics of various surfaces in the house. Also, excessive reverberation may result from raising the sound level, particularly of the low frequencies. *The response of the reinforcement system must therefore be adjusted whenever level is changed*. Initially the response is set to match the human voice at the lowest playing level as heard in the farthest seat in the house.

Procedure (high level): Pick up the speech by microphones and reproduce it from the loudspeakers located in the vertical plane of the source of sound; i.e., in the footlights in front of the performer or over his head. A single loudspeaker unit above the center of the proscenium arch will usually preserve the illusion that all sound is coming from the performer. Adjust frequency response as required.

Alternate procedure A (low level): When the ceiling is low and the house very large, as in the case of an armory, reproduced sound from above the sound source would have to be very loud at the listener locations near the stage to be heard at all in distant locations. Therefore, it is necessary to reproduce sound from loudspeakers close to the listener. Under such circumstances:

1. the microphone must be far enough away from the sound source to provide a delay or lag in the reproduced sound similar to that of the unamplified sound; or,
2. the relationship of intensity of direct to reproduced sound must be such that the audience hears very little of the direct sound; or,
3. an electronic lag mechanism must be employed to introduce a lag in the reproduced sound which is projected from loudspeakers farthest from the source.

Alternate procedure B (low level): When the house is so reverberant that any increase in level of sound makes speech progressively less understandable, loudspeakers near listener location must be used to project sound directly to the listeners. Frequencies below 500 cycles per second should be attenuated by a program equalizer to improve intelligibility, retain realism, and reduce aural fatigue in the listener.

PROBLEM 2. To reinforce a prop sound.

Procedure: Pick up by microphone and reproduce from backstage or over proscenium loudspeakers. The suspense in TEN MINUTE ALIBI is maintained by reinforcing the ticking of the clock and projecting it to the audience to bridge scene changes. The tempest in THE TEMPEST is most convincing when made with mechanical sound generators and projected electronically. Sounds can be meshed with the lines.

PROBLEM 3. To enhance a musical number by increasing the dynamics beyond what is possible with conventional instruments.

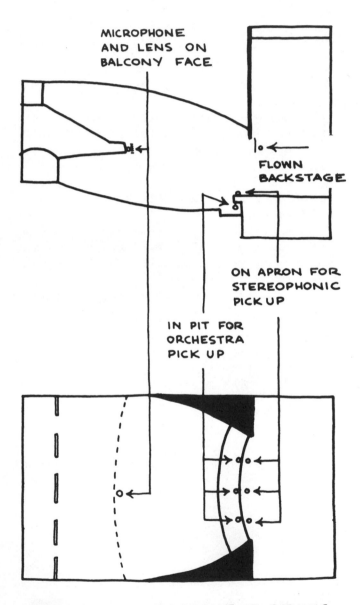

PRINCIPAL MICROPHONE POSITIONS

Microphone positions for live pickup from the stage. It is seldom necessary to use them all.

Procedure: Pick up by microphone or reproduce from record and project to audience from loudspeakers at locations from which direct or reflected sound would logically come.

Examples: The trombone passages from HUT ON FOWLS LEGS in Moussorgsky's PICTURES AT AN EXHIBITION projected at higher intensity than is possible with trombones; the Widor TOCCATA in F, reproduced with peaks of over 100 dB.

PROBLEM 4. To reproduce the auditory elements of the brainstorm sequence in Elmer Rice's THE ADDING MACHINE.

Procedure: Record separate effects on at least three tapes. Use these plus an oscillator to produce a warble note, as separate sources. On cue, introduce one after another, each from a different direction, varying the balance, build up for 30 seconds to a peak of 105 dB. Increase frequency, intensity, and rate of warble of oscillator note until it is the dominant sound at the end of the sequence. Employ loudspeakers to give the sound a nondirectional quality after the first 8 seconds. Kill on the Red Flash.

Caution: This technique can be overdone and was, when first used. The audience was almost paralyzed, and some of the patrons became very angry. Employed with discretion, however, it supplements and reinforces the visual chaos. No one forgets it and it pays off at the box office.

PROBLEM 5. To provide definition in speech or song delivered at *low intensity* in conventional theatres as in the case of the songs in LUTE SONG.

Discussion: Since the problem is not one of audibility but of understandability or definition, it is necessary to reinforce only the high frequencies above 500 cycles per second which carry the definition in speech and song. High frequencies are most effectively absorbed in air and by surface materials in the theatre, and are lost, to a large extent, out of the original signal before it reaches the audience position. The reinforcement of the highs essential to the unvoiced sounds will restore the balance between highs and lows at the listener's position.

Procedure: Pick up and project sound as in Problem 1. Attenuate the low end of the spectrum. Reproduce at an intensity which will not raise the over-all sound level in the theatre.

DYNAMICS

In 1940, the Bell Telephone Laboratories first demonstrated its system of stereophonic recording. For the public demonstration a record had been made of the Widor TOCCATA IN F performed on the organ in the Tabernacle at Salt Lake City. Played for the judges who were assembling the program, this piece was rejected as without sufficient distinction to warrant a place in the program. However, the TOCCATA recording was replayed at a level 6 dB above the original one. The judges reversed themselves, and the number was one of the best received items on the program. Episodes such as this illustrate the importance of the control of intensity of the auditory component of any dramatic episode. It has further been demonstrated that the useful range of intensity is from below the ambient noise level in the theatre (it is possible to understand speech and some other sounds at intensities below the ambient sound level) to intensities in the neighborhood of 110 dB.

During the season of 1929-30, the American Society of Mechanical Engineers sponsored a pageant to celebrate the fiftieth anniversary of the founding of that society. All music was electronically reproduced. In one episode, a musical crescendo accompanied a visual presentation of considerable dramatic power. It was observed in successive performances that the response of the audience, indicated by the extent to which they leaned forward in their seats, could be directly controlled by varying the intensity of the music at this point. The episode achieved or did not achieve the desired effect, depending upon the intensity of the music.

BALANCE

PROBLEM 6. To achieve a desired balance between instruments in the orchestra beyond what is possible with the instruments themselves.

Example A: In the overture to Offenbach's ORPHEUS the solo violin has a passage during which it is required to dominate the rest of the orchestra. If the orchestra plays down to let the violin dominate, the accompaniment sounds emasculated and distorted since instruments play their truest spectrum only at normal playing intensity. If several violins are used for a solo passage, it does not sound like a solo.

Procedure: Pick up the solo violin by microphone and reproduce with intensity enough to dominate the orchestra while the orchestra plays at normal intensity.

Example B: In the development of a crescendo in opera it is conventional for the singer to dominate the orchestra to the limit of his intensity range at which point the dynamics are taken over by the orchestra. This convention, arising from the limitations of the human voice, militates against the full effectiveness of numerous operatic passages, notably Brünnhilde's Immolation.

Procedure: By reinforcing Brünnhilde's voice so that it is able to dominate the orchestra through to the end of the vocal passage, the scene is given a presence and effectiveness not possible in the traditional production convention.

Caution: As indicated in Chapter II, when intensity is changed by electronic means, frequency compensation has to be introduced to compensate for the non-linear characteristics of the human ear.

SPECTRUM

Control of spectrum is necessary for several reasons: (1), to assure realism or conformity with any desired dramatic idiom;

(2), to compensate for acoustical characteristics of the particular house such as the absorption of certain frequencies much more rapidly than others; (3), to compensate for non-linear characteristics of the ear when sounds are reproduced at very high or very low level; (4), to adjust the spectrum to the special requirements of the play, i.e., removal of frequencies to give the sound apparent distance, suppression of frequencies to avoid interference, or synthesizing complete spectra.

PROBLEM 7. To reproduce the sound of a telephone, radio communication system, small radio, jukebox, etc.

Procedure: So long as the system has an equal or greater frequency range than the sound to be reproduced, attenuate frequencies other than those which characterize the source required in the play. The easiest way to do this is to use the actual device, i.e., a telephone receiver, the loudspeaker of the small radio. The sound, when recorded with the desired spectrum, can be made to sound convincing when reproduced through a good sound control system.

DISTORTION

PROBLEM 8. To create a sepulchral voice appropriate to an ectoplasmic figure of the ghost in HAMLET.

Procedure: Filter out the midfrequencies of the voice sharply and reinforce the ends of the spectrum. Dub the sound to the ectoplasmic figure (see Problem 31).

Comment: This technique was first demonstrated in a production in the Stevens Theatre in 1934. It has since become part of the standard electronic bag of tricks.

FREQUENCY DISCRIMINATION

PROBLEM 9: To reproduce two simultaneous sounds in such a manner that they will not interfere with each other. Clemence Dane's COME OF AGE requires background music which has considerable significance for the play but must not mask the speech. The same requirement occurs in the Pleasant Place scene in THE ADDING MACHINE. In both these problems the music must be without apparent source.

Procedure: Pick up music from record or from live orchestra and project it directly or by reflection from the house ceiling and walls and backstage. This will give the music presence and make possible an apparent level much higher than it actually is. Adjust the frequency response of the music channel to attenuate frequencies from 500 to 2500. If it is necessary to reinforce the speech, do so through a system which projects the speech from behind or above the actors and attenuate frequencies below 500 and above 2500. By manipulation of inputs only, adjust the relative intensity to a point where the understandability of speech and the intensity of music satisfy the director's requirement. Control of dynamics by output control preserves the

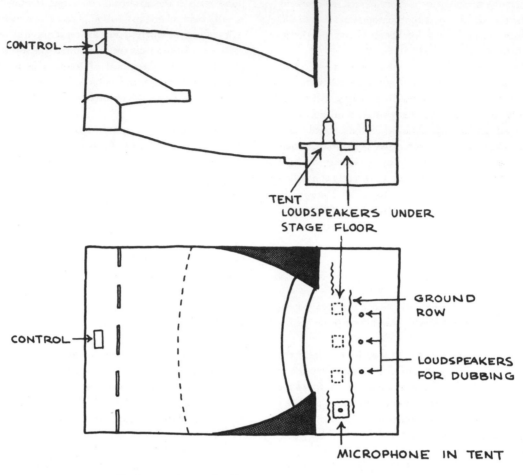

CONTROL

TENT
LOUDSPEAKERS UNDER
STAGE FLOOR

CONTROL

GROUND
ROW

LOUDSPEAKERS
FOR DUBBING

MICROPHONE IN TENT

Equipment layout for HAMLET: the ghost sequences.

balance. The analogous technique in stage lighting is proportional dimming.

Comment: This technique of projecting speech through a hole in the music makes possible the use of background music in legitimate production with as great effectiveness as is possible in motion pictures. In a small theatre where high intensities for music are not needed, reinforcement of speech may not be necessary. The dynamics possible with this system are quite impressive as indeed they need to be if the values in the two plays cited are to be exploited.

PROBLEM 10. To reproduce the sound of the jukebox without masking the speech, as required in Anita Loos' HAPPY BIRTHDAY.

Procedure: As pointed out in Chapter II, low-frequency sounds mask higher frequencies with considerable effectiveness. To play a jukebox on stage will practically guarantee that no speech will be heard because of the low-frequency grunt of the jukebox. However, the ear will fill in missing elements of a harmonic series and hear subjectively that which is actually

not projected. Therefore, attenuate the low frequencies and the principal speech frequencies of the record and reproduce the signal from a loudspeaker located in the actual prop jukebox on-stage or at a point directly upstage of it. The audience will accept such a false spectrum because the sound comes or appears to come from the visible prop jukebox, remote though the auditory resemblance be, and the actors can speak and be understood.

PROBLEM 11. To produce a sound outside the audible range for the drum in THE EMPEROR JONES in order to establish the cadence of the drum in the audience before anyone actually hears the drum.

Procedure: Filter the output of a standard prop thunder drum or thunder screen to pass nothing above 12 cycles. Reproduce the beat from a special resonator unit in the house if possible, otherwise in the fly loft. When the drum is to become audible, reduce the attenuation of the upper portion of the spectrum until the sound of the drum has the desired quality. A Helmholz resonator driven by a loudspeaker unit is perhaps the easiest subsonic projector to devise. The loudspeaker unit may need to be modified to provide adequate excursion for the voice coil and cone.

Caution: The threshold of audibility at about 12 cycles is only 4 dB above the threshold of feeling. Therefore, the level of the sound must be held within that narrow range. The hazards of this technique are noted in the reference to BERKELEY SQUARE in Chapter IV. The technique was employed with considerable success in the Stevens Theatre where the floor of the orchestra was vibrated as the sound projector.

SYNTHESIS

Though many theatrical requirements can be satisfied by attenuating parts of the sound spectrum, such techniques are limited in that you can never get anything more out of the sound than what is there to start with. By creating the sound that you want rather than modifying an existing one, it is possible to satisfy any requirement in terms of spectrum which will have any desired significance as far as the audience is concerned.

PROBLEM 12. To create voices for the witches in MACBETH which have characteristics which the human voice cannot produce but which are appropriate to the supernatural figure.

Comment: Margaret Webster first enunciated the concept that the witches might be treated as demons seen only in Macbeth's own troubled mind. Such demons should be invisible to the audience. To satisfy the requirements of the scenes in which they appear, though invisible, they should cast shadows. This treatment requires support in all elements of production, scenery, business, and light. Banquo's business and the reading of his lines lend themselves to this interpretation.

Procedure: Construct with Vocoder or Sonovox three voices, one pitched above the range of the human voice, one below voice range, and the third with a gravelly spectrum not possible in normal human speech. Record the scenes and background music needed to contribute to the mood (The scherzo from Prokofieff's CONCERTO IN C MINOR has been employed successfully for this purpose.)

Operation: Project the background music into the fly loft to give it a reverberant characteristic and make it surround the action. Project the witches' speech through three loudspeakers evenly spaced upstage of the area of movement of the witches' shadows. With director, stage manager, and electrician, synchronize the movement of the voices (by output control manipulation) with the movement of the shadows cast by the invisible witches in the movement sequences.

PROBLEM 13. MIDSUMMER NIGHT'S DREAM. To give Bottom an ass's voice during the sequence in which he wears an ass's head.

Procedure: Synthesize an ass's voice on the Vocoder using a recording of a donkey's bray as a reference. Set up the Vocoder so that the voice of the actor who plays Bottom will be used as a trigger mechanism to make the ass's voice speak. Mix in enough of the actor's own voice with the synthesized voice to maintain the identity of the character. Before setting up the Vocoder it will be observed that an ass uses a frequency range about three times that which man uses, and reaches his highest intensities at the upper and lower ends of his frequency range. Record the synthesized speeches.

Operation: Locate three loudspeakers (they need be only 3-inch loudspeakers capable of reproducing voice frequencies only, and so may be hidden inconspicuously in the scenery) evenly spaced across the stage upstage of Bottom's positions. Dub the speeches to Bottom by output control manipulation. Considerable rehearsal with the actor will be necessary for cueing, and to synchronize with Bottom's movements.

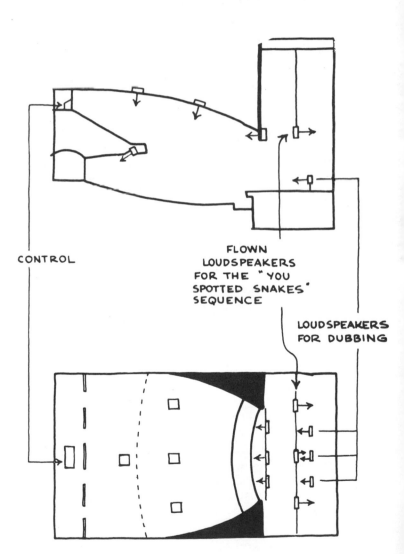

CONTROL

FLOWN LOUDSPEAKERS FOR THE "YOU SPOTTED SNAKES" SEQUENCE

LOUDSPEAKERS FOR DUBBING

Equipment layout for A MIDSUMMER NIGHT'S DREAM.

Comment: This treatment of Bottom will be accepted as completely logical by the audience, to which an actor's muffled voice coming from an ass's head has always seemed incongruous.

PROBLEM 14. THE TEMPEST. To provide Ariel with a voice conforming to Alonzo's description.

"Méthought the billows spoke and told me of it;
The winds did sing it to me, and the thunder,
That deep and dreadful organ-pipe, pronounc'd
The name of Prosper."

Procedure: Reproduce the wind and thunder as required from records for use with the Sonovox or Firestone Artificial Larynx. Record the speeches through the modifying devices. Reproduce the speech in the voices of thunder and wind from any locations the director finds appropriate as positions for the unseen Ariel. An effective location has been found to be the ceiling at the back of the house.

REVERBERATION

Reverberation control is important in establishing locale, contributing to atmosphere and mood and may be used in many arbitrary ways to enhance dramatic effect. A scene in a church should sound like a church, which a theatre generally does not.

Consciously or not, it is the habit of composers to visualize their compositions as being played in specific places. The reverberant characteristics of the place of performance then becomes a part of the music.

PROBLEM 15. To perform the Widor TOCCATA IN F in the theatre which has a short reverberation time as compared with a large church in the manner intended by the composer.

Procedure: Calculate the reverberation time of St. Sulpice where Widor was organist. Set the artificial reverberation device to provide the requisite decay pattern. Record the piece. Play it over all loudspeakers in the theatre, bringing up house loudspeakers on the crescendo. If the theatre has an organ which is adequate, pick up the organ and reproduce the reverberant portion of the signal over the house loudspeakers. Reinforce crescendo backstage if possible without feedback.

PROBLEM 16. PEER GYNT. To give a voice to the Great Boyg.

Procedure: Pick up the actor's speech by microphone, introduce reverberation, reproduce in the fly loft and at very low level in ceiling loudspeakers in the house. This arrangement gives the speech all-pervading quality and maintains the esthetic distance.

PROBLEM 17. MURDER IN THE CATHEDRAL. When a single stylized set is used to change the setting between the steps outside the cathedral and the interior of the cathedral by auditory suggestion.

Procedure: Pick up all speech in scenes, inside the cathedral and reproduce through a reverberation device. Project from loudspeakers over the proscenium and backstage. *Do not* reinforce the original sound. The reproduced reverberant sound must stay about 6 dB below the level of the original signal.

Note: Since the ear interprets variations in reverberation as dynamics, reverberation time can be increased as a substitute for increase in intensity for heightening the dramatic effect.

PROBLEM 18. To make an echo.

Procedure: Pick up the original signal and run through reverberation device which has been adjusted so that the first reproduced signal comes at the desired interval after the original signal. Project the echo from whatever direction is dramatically appropriate.

Comment: An electronic echo, since it can be controlled in spectrum and intensity, can easily be made quite absurd and is therefore useful for comic purposes.

PROBLEM 19. FAUST, the scene in the church. Herbert Graf posed two problems here: (a), to make a church scene sound like

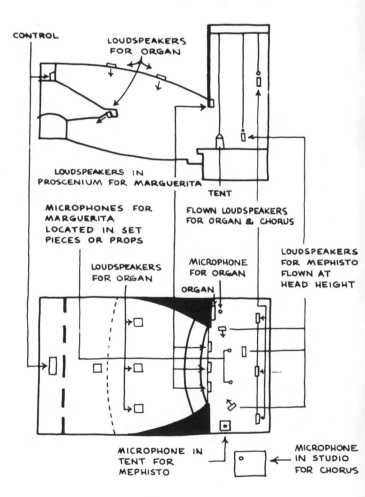

Microphone and loudspeaker positions for the church scene in FAUST.

a church, and (b), to keep Mephisto physically out of the scene. It was his contention that the physical appearance of Mephisto is a concession to the acoustic limitations of the opera house and that the scene is much more effective if only the disembodied voice of Mephisto in authoritative intensity suddenly interposes itself before Marguerita each time she tries to flee, no matter what direction she takes. Performances done in this manner have proved him right.

Procedure: Pick up the song from Marguerita by microphones planted in props or scenery. Pick up Mephisto from an offstage microphone in an enclosure or tent. Pick up organ, and pick up chorus from studio or suitable position backstage. Balance levels by input manipulation, control dynamics at the output. Project organ in fly loft. Run signal from chorus, Marguerita, and Mephisto through reverberation device. Project chorus from backstage, Mephisto's voice from planted loudspeakers set up to accord with Marguerita's business, and Marguerita's song in perspective from loudspeakers over the proscenium. The reverberation in the first phrases of Marguerita's song in which she sings *a cappella* is particularly effective in making locale convincing and establishing mood.

DISTANCE

PROBLEM 20. To give a far away characteristic to a sound as Hunding's Horn in DIE WALKÜRE or a far-off locomotive whistle. Those portions of the sound spectrum most rapidly attenuated in air must be suppressed and the sound projected at a sufficiently low level to make the distance credible. Whether a recording or an authentic instrument or a prop device is used, it is a good thing to have the source actually some distance removed from the acting area. A stage with a set in place, and others stored and flown, does a very effective job of sound absorption.

Procedure: Pick up the sound. Adjust equalizing network or frequency discrimination filter. Project from backstage loudspeakers flown above proscenium height.

PROBLEM 21. To give sound an immediacy which will be accepted as originating right outside the ear of each member of the audience or inside his own head, depending upon suggestion in the lines or business.

Procedure: Sounds which impose this requirement such as the audience eavesdropping on a telephone conversation or Jeanne d'Arc's voices must be reproduced from as many locations as possible in such a manner that the source is nondirectional. The audience must not be able to identify any source. The intimacy is a function of level and spectrum and must be developed in rehearsal.

PROBLEM 22. MADAME, WILL YOU WALK, by Sidney Howard. To provide a supernatural celestial orchestra whose music can be summoned out of nowhere to fill the theatre from an unidentifiable source.

Procedure: Record the number, project it from loudspeakers onstage and in the house so balanced that the audience cannot identify the source.

PROBLEM 23. LAZARUS LAUGHED. The complexity of the production problems posed by O'Neill in this play has deterred producers from undertaking it. It calls for several of the techniques here described. Cheryl Crawford had proposed a production scheme which, tested out, made LAZARUS LAUGHED a theatrical experience not soon forgotten. The production scheme calls for using the audience as the crowd in the amphitheatre in the last act, and modulating an organ chord for the laughter. The scene then shows Tiberius' box, with the pyre in the orchestra pit and Lazarus is heard but not seen. The light from leaping flames is the only illumination.

Procedure: Play the musical chord or figure on an organ, pick it up by microphone and, using Vocoder, Sonovox or Firestone Artificial Larynx, convert it into laughter, using the actor's own laughter as the trigger mechanism. Record the laughter, mixing some of the actor's own voice with the synthesized laughter, to preserve identity. Since no voice is capable of the sustained laughter called for, the record must be made in sections. Quality changes must be timed to the running schedule of the sequence. The quality of the last sequence must be sustained and recorded several minutes over normal running time to allow for performances that run long. The laughter of Lazarus, then is heard first from the pit, then by the addition of loudspeakers in the fly loft, from above and around the Emperor's box, and finally above the house.

Record the chants and cheering of the crowd. Reproduce at the appropriate level nondirectionally in the house so that each member of the audience is willing to accept the proposition that he is a member of the shouting, cheering, chanting mob.

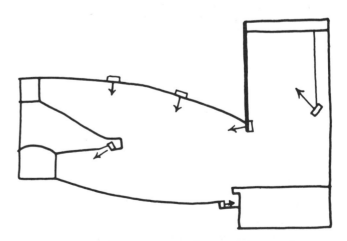

Loudspeaker positions for LAZARUS LAUGHED. Three loudspeakers are rigged on an upstage pipe and three set in the pit.

DIRECTION

Control of the apparent direction and the apparent distance of sound is often involved in the same theatrical problem as illustrated above. In the simplest form:

PROBLEM 24. To enable the audience in the Metropolitan Opera House to hear the pipe organ from stage left as demanded by several operas instead of stage right where it is.

Procedure: Pick up the organ by microphone, reproduce it from loudspeakers stage left.

Comment: As long as the level of sound originating from stage left is as great as the original sound of the organ from right, the audience will accept the left as the point of origin if there is any visual indication that that is where the sound should be coming from.

PROBLEM 25. THE LIVING NEWSPAPER. To provide a voice. The voice of the living newspaper was an essential element of that idiom which found such wide application after its introduction in the 1930s. The disembodied voice had to be part of the show and yet not identifiable as to direction.

Procedure: Locate the actor in a projection booth or at some other point out front where he can see as well as hear all the production. Reproduce his speech through loudspeakers located all the way across the top of the proscenium.

PROBLEM 26. MARY ROSE. To make the voices calling Mary Rose progressively more insistent.

Procedure: Record the voices.

Operation: As the voices become more insistent, increase the area from which they are projected, i.e., first backstage loudspeakers, then proscenium loudspeakers, then house loudspeakers, keeping the level so low as to make it credible that characters on stage aside from Mary Rose should not hear the sound, but allowing the audience to feel the immediacy and insistence of the call.

PROBLEM 27. HAPPY BIRTHDAY, by Anita Loos. To make a cash register play a tune and a bottle speak.

Procedure: Pick up the music from a tape record or by microphone from an instrument, and the speech by microphone. Project each signal from a loudspeaker built into the set upstage of the cash register and just below the bottle. The attention is directed to apparent sources by lighting each up when sound is to come from it.

Note: The audience's inability to locate sound sources in the vertical plane makes possible the use of a single loudspeaker.

MOVEMENT

Directional control of sound was strikingly demonstrated in the Federal Theatre Production "1935" when an airplane was made to circle above the audience. This effect is achieved by projecting the sound from successive loudspeakers. If the loudspeakers are not more than 30 deg. apart from the audience position, the sound may be made to appear to come from any point between any two loudspeakers by adjusting the relative intensity of output to the loudspeakers. By attenuating one while bringing up the other, the sound may be made to appear to move from one to the other. One feature of stereophonic recording first demonstrated by the Bell Laboratories in 1940 is that sound may be made to move about the stage by using a multitrack record. However, for legitimate productions, due to the variation in pace from performance to performance, it is best to accomplish movement of sound manually. All the loudspeakers must be in phase if this method is to be effective.

PROBLEM 28. Any play with a railroad train in it.

Procedure: Set up three loudspeakers behind the scenery in a line across the stage or hung above the set and projecting by reflection from the stage floor. Set output control in the loudspeaker line at the side where the effect is to start, at the desired level for maximum intensity in that line. To start, build up input to operating level. When this point has been reached, build up second loudspeaker line to a point 4 dB below the first loudspeaker output and take out the first one while continuing to build up line No. 2 to desired level. Repeat to shift from line No. 2 to line No. 3. Conclude the effect by taking out input.

PROBLEM 29. THE TEMPEST. For Ariel (unseen) to fly about playing his tabor and pipe and finally lead Stephano and Trincolo away to the other side of the island.

Procedure: Record the tabor and pipe and reproduce by the technique described in Problem 28 from loudspeakers in desired sequence above the audience and backstage. An acceptable routine is to have the tabor and pipe fade in backstage right and have Ariel circle the house above the audience twice and then fade out upstage left, followed by Trincolo and Stephano.

PROBLEM 30. TANNHAUSER. To make the Pilgrims' Chorus move.

Procedure: Pick up the chorus by microphones hung backstage and concealed on the apron. Project the song progressively from loudspeakers which reflect the sound from the side wall of the house so that the chorus appears to move down one side of the theatre and out on to the stage as the live chorus enters. Reinforce the Alleluias from loudspeakers over the proscenium.

Caution: Careful gain riding is necessary to avoid abrupt change in level when the chorus comes onstage and pickup shifts to microphones on the apron or hung from the first pipe.

DUBBING

As indicated in previous problems, there are many theatrical requirements for sound to come from a source which cannot produce it, as the statue in ALCESTE, the prop lyre in ORFEO.

PROBLEM 31. To make possible an aside which is heard by the audience but not spoken by the actor, as in Elmer Rice's THE ADDING MACHINE or Eugene O'Neill's STRANGE INTERLUDE.

The aside is a convention to let the audience eavesdrop on the thinking of the character. He thinks in several voices in THE ADDING MACHINE, in only his own in STRANGE INTERLUDE.

Procedure: Pick up speech from a voice double or a tape recording of the actor's voice, and project it from a point upstage of the actor. This problem is simple in the case of the operatic voice provided for Addie Bemis in HAPPY BIRTHDAY in which the singer's position does not change. Similarly, in Robinson Jeffers' TOWER BEYOND TRAGEDY, the voice of Agamemnon is projected from Cassandra who remains in one position during the sequence. For Bottom (Problem 13), movement is involved and the technique described in Problem 28 must be used to follow the actor with his voice as with a follow spot.

ACOUSTIC ENVELOPE

Singers and solo instrumentalists prefer to perform in a reasonably reverberant place because the ability to hear themselves clearly helps to insure against technical errors. Large theatres with large audiences present often do not have the acoustical characteristics that make for optimum performance. The sound goes away from the performer, and stays away. It is therefore desirable to make it possible for the performer to hear himself onstage as he does in the studio.

PROBLEM 32. To surround the performer onstage with conditions acoustically similar to a small studio.

Procedure: Pick up the performer by microphone, filter out all frequencies below 500 cycles and project via directional loudspeaker to the performer from a distance greater than that of the first reflected sound, i.e., to the floor and back. The projection must be highly directional to avoid feedback. It can be at such low level that persons other than the performer within its range will not notice it.

Acoustic Envelope: Loudspeaker and amplifier in place behind the proscenium, stage right, at Carnegie Hall.

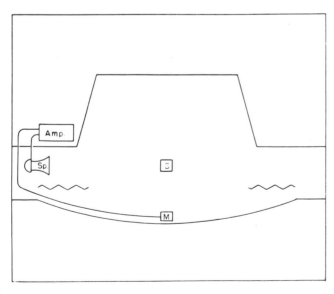

Acoustic Envelope.

GENERAL COMMENT

As indicated in the foregoing two chapters, there are readily available techniques by which practically any auditory requirement connected with the show can be met. It is therefore incumbent upon playwrights and composers to take advantage of the medium. It is difficult to give an imaginative treatment to sound which is conventionally conceived in the first instance. It is encouraging to note that some of the best creative work in the theatre is now being done with a view to electronic enhancement of the sound. The late Kurt Weill composed the music for MADAM, WILL YOU WALK with a view to the limitations of the electronic equipment to be used. There was nothing significant in the score which required over 10,000-cycle reproduction. Richard Rodgers and Robert Russell Bennett have both been at pains to explore the sound control implications for the musical elements of scores which they were composing to avoid pitfalls and make provision for exploiting the increased flexibility which electronic control affords to music.

CHAPTER VI

SYSTEMS

Thus far, this book has derived from the necessities of the production, the nature of sound sources and pickup facilities, loudspeaker placement, and the types of control required. This chapter will develop the basic specifications for electronic sound control systems based on previously stated requirements.

Many theatres have electronic sound reinforcing systems which provide excellent audibility, but permanently installed systems which provide the flexibility of control required by some of the productions cited in Chapter V are rare. Few old theatres have sound control stations at the rear of the house, or studios suitable for pickup, or even adequate facilities for loudspeaker placement. Because of these inadequacies productions requiring electronic sound control carry their own equipment, as in the case of lights, and are forced to improvise loudspeaker and control locations. Whether or not an installed system is available, the play dictates the type and capability of system required.

TYPES OF SYSTEMS

Requirements so far set forth are met by three systems:

1. A simple reenforcement (PA) system to provide even distribution of speech and/or music at the desired level over the whole audience.
2. A system for adjusting the sound to suit the performance by change of reverberation time, spectrum and level of reflected sound. (Royal Festival Hall) This system may use mechanics as well as electronic devices.
3. A theatre sound control system which can exercise complete control over the audio component of the production as required by the production: a multichannel electronic system which can handle the problems exemplified in Chapter V.

These systems can consist of various combination of equipment and different types of installation. The maxim "To make it good, make it simple" applies here. An absolute imperative!

EQUIPMENT CHARACTERISTICS

Electronic sound equipment for theatrical use must be of the highest electronic and mechanical sensitivity to accommodate the wide range of signal levels generated by modern microphones and microphone systems. This includes the output of the older low output dynamic microphones up through the high level output from the preamplifiers associated with modern capacitor microphones.

The use of transistors and integrated circuits (IC's) has eliminated the problem of the microphonics traditional with the electron tube preamplifiers of the past era. However, transistors and IC's must have their circuitry designed to take the extremely wide range of input levels without any special line attenuators or transformers. Some microphones with high level inputs (the nightclub singer nuzzling the microphone) can produce outputs as high as 0.02 volt. This will easily overload many of the conventional semiconductor circuits. Where special care in design has been taken the result will usually be satisfactory.

In power output amplifier circuits, there are again differences between the old-time tube amplifiers. Although transistors provide many benefits, the results may fall short of those achieved by the earlier tube systems. This is true of peak overloads. Peak overload conditions are common in speech and music dynamics. Thus a 200-watt transistor amplifier is needed to handle the peaks for which a 50-watt tube amplifier was formerly adequate. In the jargon of the engineer, the tube amplifier overloaded gently while the transistor amplifiers cut off or square off the signal under overload conditions.

The operating characteristics of transistor amplifiers also

make them quite susceptible to low level distortion, almost unheard of in electron tube designs. The use of large quantities of inverse feedback does not relieve these problems completely. It is therefore necessary to choose equipment carefully, examining the distortion versus output data as well as the maximum ratings.

Another problem with power transistors has been their tendency toward self-destruction under improper load conditions. Almost all commercial grade equipment sold today is equipped with short-circuit protection. Electron tube equipment was known to blow fuses under long term short circuit conditions, but was much more forgiving of short term overloads and short circuits.

Experience with theatre, nightclub and hotel presentation sound systems has led to the conclusion that semiconductor sound systems must have adequate redundancy of components to permit patching or switching in a new unit during the show to replace one that has quit.

BASIC ELEMENTS

All electronic sound control systems consist of the same basic elements:

1. Inputs or sources and associated amplifiers to step up the signal.
2. Networks for mixing and switching inputs to program channels. (The number of channels is determined by the number of simultaneous and independent programs.)
3. Provision for switching outputs to program channels.
4. Outputs.

SINGLE CHANNEL

A single-channel system without switching (items 2 and 3) will satisfy most public address requirements and the demands of many legitimate theatrical productions. It will provide simple reinforcement (Chapter V, Problem 1), backstage effects (Problem 3), manually enhanced dynamics and orchestral balance (Problem 6), and localization of sound (Problem 24). It can make it possible for the performer to hear himself (Problem 32).

SINGLE CHANNEL SYSTEM

HIGH-LEVEL, LOW-LEVEL REINFORCEMENT

In a high-level system the location of source can easily be maintained. The sound comes from above or occasionally below the performer, and the sound is actually raised in level. Excellent examples are the Radio City Music Hall and Madison Square Garden. High-level is the most common, and in its stereophonic form, the best form of reinforcement.

When reverberation is excessive, as is often the case in an armory, large church, or exposition hall, raising the level of sound will start reverberation and make speech unintelligible. If the ceiling is low and the auditorium is so large that some members of the audience are almost a hundred yards closer to the stage than others, a high-level system would drive the audience out of the first rows, while patrons in or under the balconies could not hear satisfactorily. To overcome the limitations imposed by low ceiling or long reverberation time, or both, loudspeakers must be placed close to the audience in the ceiling under the balcony and sometimes in the face of the stage apron, and operated at low level. To cover a large audience, many loudspeakers are required, operating at a level at which each member of the audience hears only the loudspeaker nearest to him.

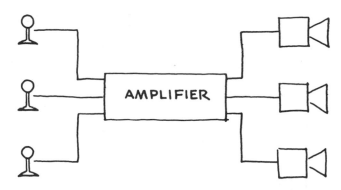

Single-channel system with multiple inputs and outputs.

A low-level system is still the simple single-channel system with a number of loudspeakers driven by the power amplifier or amplifiers. When pickup must come from the whole stage, a number of microphones is required.

The low-level reinforcement system assures adequate level for speakers, soloists, and small ensembles. The acoustical design, architectural and electronic, of the Jorgensen auditorium of the University of Connecticut here illustrated was undertaken as a unit. It was, therefore, possible to provide optimum reverberation time for music by architectural means, and distribution of speech electronically.

Another notable example was a low-level system applied to a hotel dining room: the former Persian Room in the Hotel

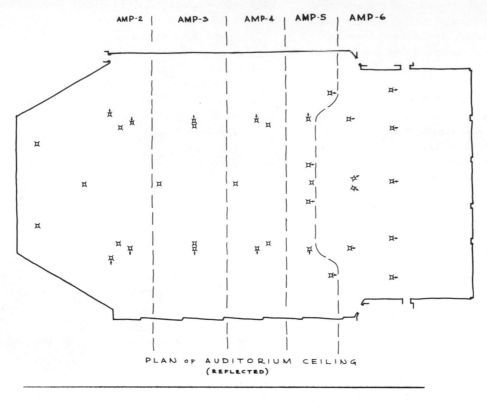

PLAN OF AUDITORIUM CEILING
(REFLECTED)

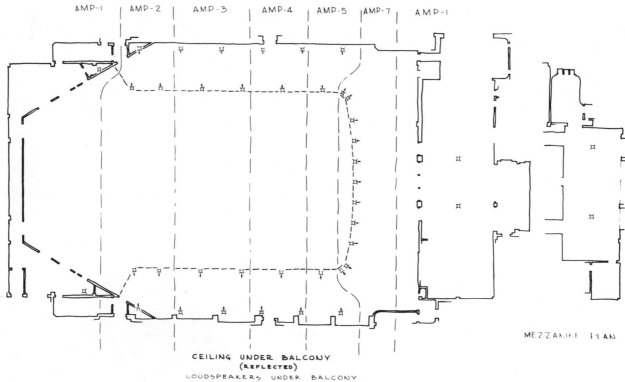

CEILING UNDER BALCONY
(REFLECTED)
LOUDSPEAKERS UNDER BALCONY

MEZZANINE PLAN

Reflected ceiling and under-balcony plans for the Auditorium of the University of Connecticut; this is an elaborate low-level system. Loudspeakers are grouped by distance from the stage to provide increasing level of reinforcement as the original sound diminishes.

Plaza, in which the sound need not appear to be reinforced at all (when the microphone is correctly used), and where phase interference is avoided by having the reinforcing loudspeakers as far away from the patrons as is the original sound source.

It is obvious that a high-level system is easier and cheaper to install than a low-level system which requires many loudspeakers and much wiring. A high-level system can be made portable and is preferred for trouping if the show and the architecture of the theatres permit it.

MULTICHANNEL SYSTEMS

Three or more independent single channels can provide stereophonic reinforcement through loudspeakers above the proscenium opening. This principle was first demonstrated by the Bell Telephone Laboratories at the Hollywood Bowl. Stereophonic reinforcement is by all odds the most satisfactory reinforcement principle. It preserves the unity of source.

The usefulness of a multichannel system is not confined to stereophonic reinforcement. In its simplest form such a system has a single input and a number of outputs. This arrangement can make the sound appear undirectional (Problems 11, 16, 22), and by relative output alternation can provide movement (Problems 28, 29, 30).

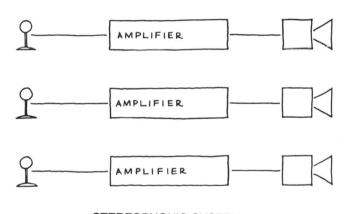

STEREOPHONIC SYSTEM

To do two jobs simultaneously, two independent single-channel systems can be used (Problem 9).

To further increase the flexibility and usefulness of a sound-control system, the next step obviously is to associate two or more program channels with a mixing network so that each channel may be fed to any or all of a number of loudspeakers or groups of loudspeakers. This basic principle fills the system requirements for the most complex problems in Chapter V. It is here illustrated in a block diagram from a multichannel system, whose specifications were derived from the operation re-

quirements of many productions, including those described in Problems 12, 13, 14, 19, 23, and 25.

The number and arrangement of channels govern the number of sound sources which can be employed simultaneously, but independently, and the location and movement of the apparent sound source as the audience hears it. Between original source—microphone or record—and loudspeaker, other types of control must be provided.

CONTROL OF INTENSITY AND DYNAMICS

Dynamics includes all types of intensity control from simple gain riding for a lecturer to complex control of balance so necessary in opera and orchestral music. The following examples illustrate the nature and necessary location in the system of a facility for dynamic control:

1. For balance of a number of sound sources, or for progressive changing of relative intensity (Problems 4, 23), control must be exercised in the input line. This control may be remote at a point where the operator can hear as the audience hears.
2. For master control of over-all intensity, preserving the relative input levels (Problem 4), control must be exercised in each program channel. This control may also be remote.
3. For control of individual loudspeakers, the output section of the system is the obvious point of control, and for purely technical reasons the output line is the best location.

FREQUENCY

Chapter V lists technical and dramatic reasons (Problems 1, 5, 8, 9, 10, 11) for frequency discrimination. Since such discrimination applies to the source of the sound, and numerous sources may be employed in the same show, each requiring different frequency discrimination, the necessary controls are most conveniently located in the input lines. Where elaborate frequency discrimination is required, special networks can be introduced into the input line or program channel.

REVERBERATION

The simplest system for synthesizing reverberation (Problems 15, 16, 17, 18, 19) is by a delayed playback device introduced into the input line or the program channel. Commercial all-electronic reverberation synthesizers are available. Ideally the reverberant sound should be controllable in three or more frequency ranges to simulate real conditions in some

Foil Electromechanical Reverberation Generator (Gotham Audio Corp.).

Electrodynamic Reverberation Unit.

locations or give desired distinction to the basic signal. Failing this, any highly reverberant chamber, vault, or elevator shaft may be used; one channel terminates in a loudspeaker in the reverberation chamber, and another picks up the signal by a microphone in that chamber and terminates in the loudspeaker which projects sound to the audience. Sound projected into a live fly loft will be reverberant when the audience hears it.

LOCATION

The problems set forth in Chapter V require in most instances, that the sound-control operator be able to see and hear the show as the audience sees and hears it. This is recognized in modern theatre architecture by the provision of a sound-control station at the back of the house beside the projection booth. In old theatres, booths are sometimes improvised, or operation is from a box or the orchestra pit. Backstage operation is tolerable for effects when level is not critical, but for consistent good operation, the operator must be in the open.

CONTROL

Operation of any system requires a number of controls. To have these visible and within easy reach of the operator requires that those which are most used—input and output gain controls, and channel switches—be assembled on a single panel. Frequency discrimination controls and patching or push-button facilities for shifting speaker or microphone lines in the rare event of amplifier failure, may well stay on the amplifier chassis or the racks. These controls are required only in setup and emergency, and not in the operation of the show.

In very large auditoriums the sound-control booth is often so far from the critical audience location that remote control of intensity is necessary. This is, in effect, split control with one operator handling setup and such operation as does not require close audience contact, and the other, with a portable console, sitting in the audience controlling cues and level. The portable console duplicates the input controls of the line or program channel.

SUMMARY

Required characteristics of a system, then, are:
1. Enough input lines to make it unnecessary to move microphones during the show.
2. A gain control for each input.
3. Remote controls so that an operator can sit in the audience when necessary.
4. Frequency-equalization networks so that the spectrum of each input signal can be equalized or adjusted to specification at this point without affecting any other element in the system.
5. Master controls with which total level can be controlled while preserving the relative levels of various inputs (Problem 4). The parallel in stage lighting control is proportional dimming.
6. Channel-level indicators by which levels can be read independently of output-control settings, and with which each channel can be tested before cue.
7. Provision for input switching to make it possible to associate any input or number of inputs with any channel.

8. Provision for introducing frequency discrimination or reverberation.
9. Provision for output switching to make it possible to associate any output or group of outputs with any channel.

PORTABILITY

The optimum portable system is a modular system, adjustable to the demands of any show without redesign. As long as a system is specially built for each show (and this is a too-common practice), it is difficult and expensive to make rehearsal changes, and performance will have some shortcomings.

Permanently installed, completely flexible systems are indicated as desiderata. Where these are not available, the producer must be prepared to pay for sound at a scale comparable to the cost of the lights that go with the show, if he expects comparable effectiveness.

The portable Sound Control System in the orchestra pit of the old Metropolitan Opera House.

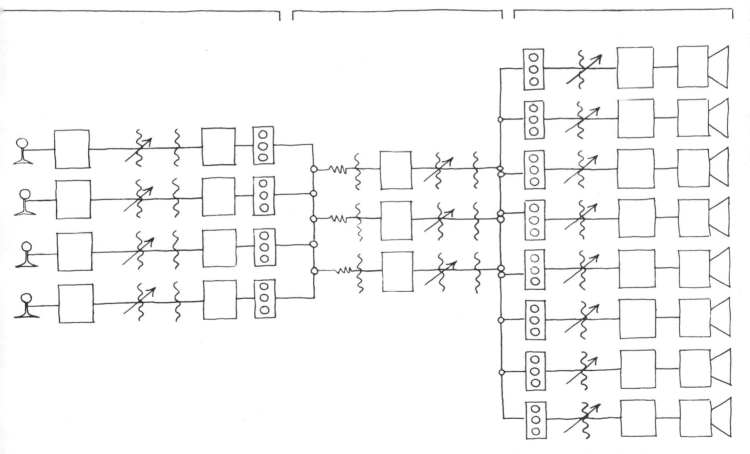

The Stevens Sound Control System, Mark 1, designed by Vincent Mallory, provides facilities for complete control of the auditory component of the show. Expansion to a four channel system is simple and may be convenient though not necessarily essential for some productions. The system here illustrated handled all the problems listed in Chapter V.

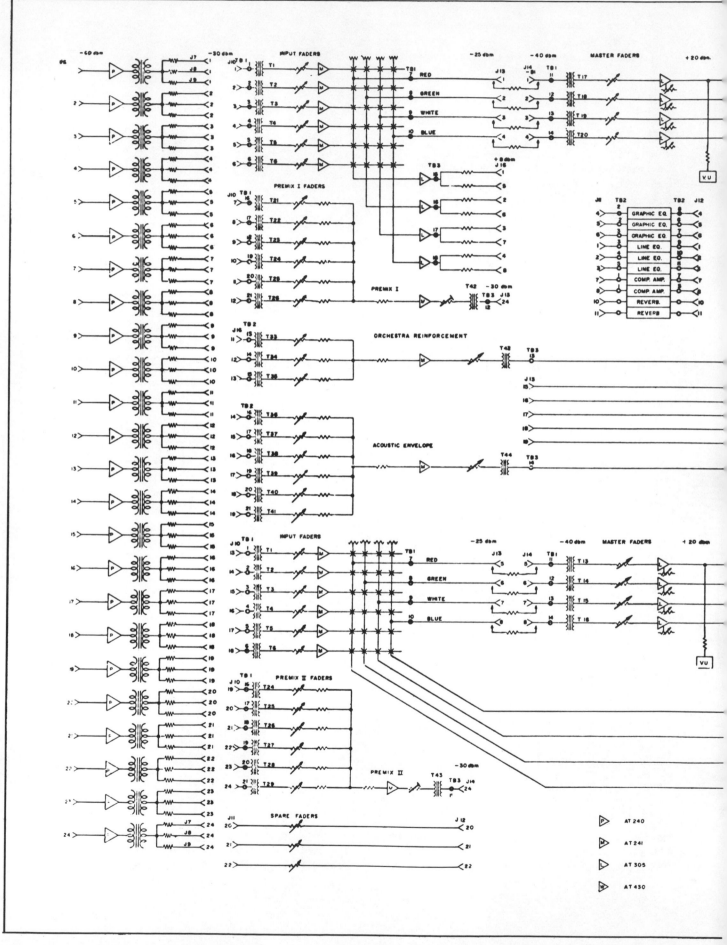

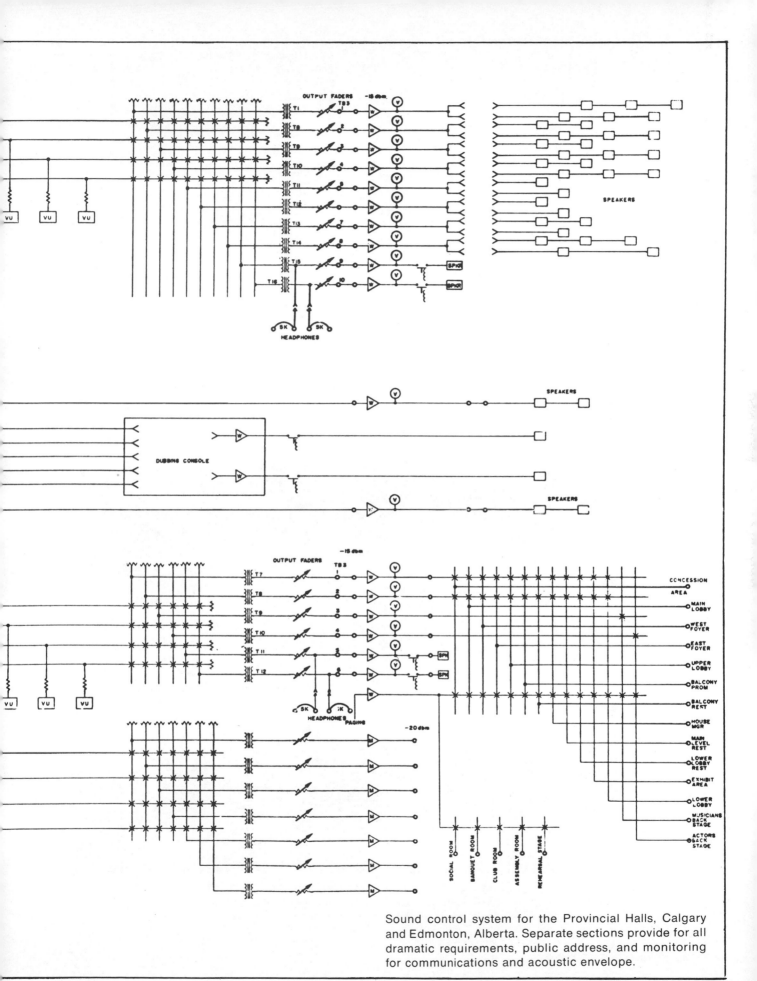

Sound control system for the Provincial Halls, Calgary
and Edmonton, Alberta. Separate sections provide for all
dramatic requirements, public address, and monitoring
for communications and acoustic envelope.

PERMANENT INSTALLATIONS

The need for sound reinforcement is generally recognized. Simple reinforcement systems can be designed with the theatre, and be part of the original equipment. It is sometimes hard to provide for complete sound-control equipment in the building budget. After all, many productions need little or none. However, it is important that the complete installation be planned and the architectural provisions made therefor, when the theatre is planned and built. The equipment can be added as it is needed, or as funds become available. This principle applies to sound-control facilities as surely as it does to rigging, stage machinery, stage lighting equipment, and to the theatre building itself. Design it right, design it all. Build only what can be built correctly. Install what you can of the right equipment, and no other.

Translated into building requirements, then the building should contain:

1. A central sound-control station at the back of the house with provision for control from the audience.
2. Loudspeaker mounting provisions in the ceiling and proscenium.

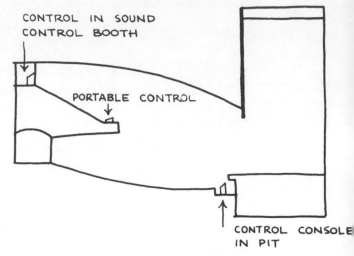

Control Locations.

3. Microphone outlets in the footlights and backstage.
4. The necessary conduits.

If these requirements are met, there will be no waste effort in bringing in and using portable equipment, or building up permanent equipment a unit at a time.

Sound Control Console Provincial Halls, Calgary and Edmonton, Alberta. Left to right: tape reproducer, control for dramatic requirements, public address, and communications.

CHAPTER VII

EQUIPMENT: OUTPUT SECTION AND CONTROLS

ONE OF THE PRINCIPAL IMPEDIMENTS to the extension of electronic sound control has been the mistaken notion that almost any kind of electronic equipment will do. It won't.

Here are presented the basic essential elements of equipment necessary to accomplish the most exacting task.

TYPES OF EQUIPMENT

At present, three types of high-quality sound amplifying and reproducing equipment are available. The first of these is the familiar and popular component-high-fidelity set used and enjoyed in many homes. It is simply and straightforwardly designed to do its job, with a minimum of switching and control. Bulk, weight, and cost are serious considerations. Therefore single units or perhaps two units joined by relatively short unbalanced lines are the rule. Such equipment may be purchased from any neighborhood hi-fi dealer.

The second type of equipment is one that is less known to the general public. It is the professional broadcast type of equipment, designed for continuous day-to-day operation in the mixing and switching of programs. Such equipment is usually sold through manufacturer's agents and engineering firms whose names can be obtained from the manufacturer. The third category is commercial professional audio equipment.

Why don't designers of theatre sound systems use modern high fidelity sound equipment? The specifications for much of the equipment especially amplifiers and loudspeakers look so much better than the specifications for the commercial grade equipment used in theatre sound control systems. The same question is also asked with regard to broadcast grade equipment. The answer in both cases is that the commercial grade equipment used in the theatre has different requirements from those of home or broadcast grade equipment. The design life should be longer than for home equipment, the temperature rise within the unit and of the transformers must be lower for

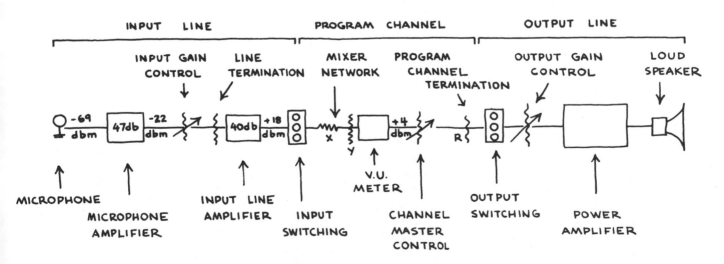

Single Channel of Sound Control System

commercial use, and the input circuits must be matched to the purpose. Broadcast grade gear is excellent and has often been used for theatre sound systems, but again input and output circuitry is designed for the broadcast system and does not readily lend itself to theatre system application. Also small but important differences occur in the allowable tolerances for distortion and response between the three grades of equipment. After many years of trying to make use of equipment designed for other services, most theatre sound system designers have settled on the highest quality of professional audio equipment for their clients. One other critical facet is frequency response of the finished equipment. Today, high fidelity system amplifiers with considerable power handling capacity are available with nominal frequency response out to 100,000 Hz or beyond. Such a wide range response is not needed nor is it really suitable for theatre sound control systems. Loudspeakers equipped with horns that provide extremely high frequency response are also unnecessary and even undesirable in theatre systems. They increase the noise output, will radiate any amplifier distortion products and make very little contribution to the auditory element of the show. Systems having a response reasonably flat out to about 15,000 Hz will be accepted by the audience during a three to four hour production.

If it were in their home such a system would probably be widely accepted although a few people might find that after long periods of listening, they preferred a system with wider response.

The hazards of using an extra-wide range system far outweigh the supposed benefits.

Loudspeakers for theatre sound use must be wide range units having separate high and low frequency sections, but home high fidelity loudspeakers are usually neither suitable nor appropriate. Broadcast monitor and theatre loudspeakers are so readily available today that their omission cannot be excused.

When a play requires the reproduction of a single sound, from a single-point source, the first type of equipment may be used (Problems 1, 3, 6, 24, 32). However, when the demands of the production or repertoire of productions become complex or when a multiplicity of sounds is required, the operational problem approaches that of a broadcast system. The simplest engineering answer to this problem is to use audio equipment of the class developed specifically for professional audio use.

Professional broadcast audio equipment is assembled from fixed-gain low-power amplifiers, coupled by low-level balanced, transformer isolated low-impedance lines. Use of these lines prevents high-frequency loss, allows components of the equipment to be operated at considerable distance from each other and provides points for the insertion of equipment to furnish gain and spectrum control. The use of low-impedance equipment further permits mixing and switching in and out of the circuit without interference, cross talk, or induced or conducted hum. The standard impedance of coupling lines is 600 ohms, except in the case of microphones which may be 30, 50, or 250 ohms.

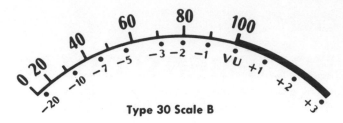

Type 30 Scale B

VU meter scale. (*Weston Electrical Instrument Company*)

To furnish these low impedances each fixed gain amplifier is equipped with input and output isolating transformers. Plate-to-grid or cathode-follower coupling common to home hi-fi sets is eliminated, thus avoiding switching transients (clicks) which result from capacitor discharge in unisolated circuits.

Each power or preliminary amplifier, if possible, should be complete in itself. Each should have its own power supply. If this is not practicable, as in the case of some preliminary amplifiers, a standby power supply must be included in the design. Each source, such as microphone, phonograph or tape reproducer, must be equalized to provide a flat output. Equalization in one part of the system to compensate for a defect in another part of the system is not good practice.

Controls are inserted into the standard lines between preliminary and power amplifiers at the point which provides the greatest degree of control with lowest distortion and noise.

Another reason for the use of professional equipment is its reliability. Failure of a component part or the sudden appearance of noise in a gain control can be taken in stride by the owner and displayer of home equipment. If repairs are not immediately possible, his disappointed guests can turn to bridge, to television, or even to the almost forgotten art of conversation. But if sound equipment fails in a play which seriously depends on sound control, cash must be refunded.

VU METER

In order to exercise control a fixed reference must first be established. The VU meter, standard for radio and recording, supplies this reference.

This meter has been designed for uniform ballistic characteristics, i.e., a standardized indicator speed and a standardized amount of overswing. It provides the operator with a familiar reference which is uniform in all correctly made installations and from meter to meter. This uniformity depends on precise compliance with the manufacturer's installation instructions. Unless specially designed, the VU meter must not be mounted on a panel of magnetic material. Circuits furnished in this book should be used as indicated. For operator's convenience it is recommended that the type "B" scale be used. This scale is calibrated both in percent and in VU with the percent scale given greater prominence. 100 percent is Zero VU. Indications from 20 to 100 percent are clearly visible. Allowance is made for an overswing of 3 dB.

When installed in a 600-ohm line, the meter with the required 3600-ohm series resistance will indicate 0 at a level of plus 4 dBm which equals 2.5 milliwatts (1.228 volts), and full scale at plus 7 dBm which equals 5 milliwatts (1.732 volts). (dBm = decibels in relation to a standard level of one milliwatt in a 600-ohm line.)

The reason for the selection of this power and voltage level as a point of reference is easily understandable. At the source (microphone or phonograph) the signal is too minute for measurement without calibrated amplifiers. At the loudspeaker the levels will vary from average room noise (about 40 dB) to full output (100 dB or more). To measure a signal intensity at this point would require a meter range of over 60 dB. The VU meter shows a readable scale of 23 dB. To show a greater range would require more complicated equipment and at least one more operator.

Inspection of the characteristics of associated equipment will show further reasons for the selection of 0 VU as the point of reference. For example, one of the most suitable of output power amplifiers requires an input of plus 2 dBm for full output. A maximum indicated level of plus 3 VU (plus 7 dBm) furnishes a margin of 5 decibels. This margin permits adjustment of gain within the power amplifier (see section on power amplifiers) to compensate for small variations of gain which sometimes result when amplifiers are replaced.

Suitable line amplifiers (ahead of the meter) are designed to furnish a maximum level of either plus 18 or plus 20 dBm.

(See section on line amplifiers.) This allows a margin of 11 to 13 decibels for losses in mixing networks.

The philosophy of operations, then, is this: Small source signals are amplified and controlled by suitable equipment shown in the block diagram, to 0 VU level. Further amplification and control are furnished to bring up the level to the maximum capacity of the loudspeaker. The controls, which are calibrated, permit the operator to set levels to satisfy the director and to reset these levels accurately at each performance.

PROGRAM CHANNEL

In each program channel, the location of the VU meter is also the most advantageous point to install switching and mixing facilities. At 0 VU the slight noise introduced by

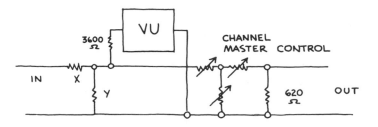

DETAIL OF MIXING NETWORK AND PROGRAM CHANNEL, SCHEMATIC

switching and control contacts is many dB below the signal level and is therefore not audible. Distortion is avoided by designing the circuit and its incidental losses in such a way that the capabilities of the preceding line amplifiers are never exceeded.

SWITCHING

An input switch must be furnished for each input line. Each switch must contain as many positions or conditions as there are channels in the system.

Optimum is a push-button switch which makes and also breaks contacts when buttons are pressed. One button at a time may be depressed or all buttons may be in the disconnect position.

The normal arrangement of a typical switch is to have all buttons interlocked by means of a common latch bar. Depressing any button automatically releases all other buttons which are depressed at the time. Therefore two or even three buttons can be latched if pressed simultaneously, resulting in serious cross talk. This mishandling of the switch however is not easy, and will be immediately evident if pilot lights are used to indicate switching conditions.

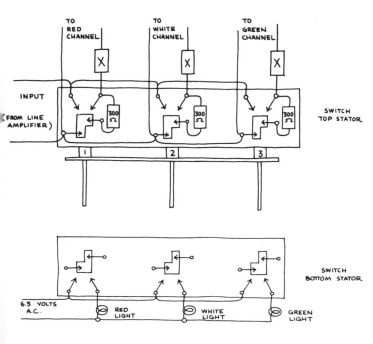

INPUT SWITCH WIRING

It is recommended that one side of the double-sided switch be used for signal-channel switching and that the opposite side be used for pilot-light switching. When distinctively colored pilot lights are used switching conditions can be read at a glance even in a blackout. Pilot lights, LED's, and buttons are available in a number of colors. Associated pilot lights and buttons should be the same color.

MIXING NETWORKS AND LOSSES

Following the input switch, a mixing network is inserted into the system. This network provides constant loading for every source, active or inactive, and this prevents changes in program level when additional sources are switched in and out. The mixing network is designed to operate preceding equipment at its best operating point and thus minimizes noise and distortion. Available line amplifiers have a maximum output of either plus 18 or plus 20 dBm. Operating the first of these at plus 15 dBm and the second at plus 17 dBm allows the customary margin of 3 decibels for overswing.

The mixing network is resistive to prevent frequency distortion. It consists of two resistors—resistor X in series with the upper conductor of the program channel and resistor Y in shunt, as shown in the associated diagram. Resistor values vary with the number of input lines. A network is needed for each channel. Resistor values are shown below.

MIXING NETWORKS

Number of input lines	X	Y	loss	Input line Maximum level
2	430 ohms	360 ohms	10.85 db	17.85 dbm
3	430 ohms	750 ohms	10.85 db	17.85 dbm
4	430 ohms	—	10.85 db	17.85 dbm
5	450 ohms	—	12.30 db	19.30 dbm
6	470 ohms	—	13.66 db	20.66 dbm

It is recommended that 5 percent, 1-watt composition resistors be used and they be mounted on terminal strips such as Cinch-Jones No. 4-141-W. The terminal strips can also provide space for mounting the necessary 3600-ohm, 5 percent, 1-watt series resistor for the VU meter.

CHANNEL MASTER LEVEL CONTROL

The next item in the program channel is the *Channel Master Level Control*. This control is a T attenuator of zero insertion loss and permits the fading in and out of the signal in the program channel. A twenty-step vertical attenuator is recommended. Each of the twenty steps reduces signal level by 2 dB.

Cueing positions on attenuators are neither necessary nor desirable in theatre sound systems. When it is necessary for the

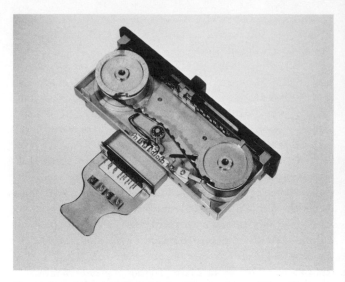

Linear Level Control Suitable for Theatre Sound Use (Gotham Audio Corp.).

operator to listen in on a program channel prior to switching that channel to an output line, headphones may be shunted across the input terminals of the channel master control.

To terminate the channel properly, a 5 percent, 1-watt Allen-Bradley or Ohmite resistor with a value of 620 ohms should be soldered across the output terminals of the Channel Master Control.

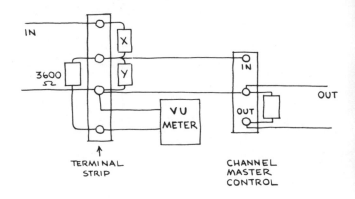

DETAIL OF MIXING NETWORK AND PROGRAM CHANNEL ASSEMBLY

OUTPUT SWITCHING

Output switching is provided by the same type of push-button switch as that used for input switching. One switch assembly is needed for each output line and must contain as many push buttons (or switch conditions) as there are program channels. Color coding and indicator light arrangements are the

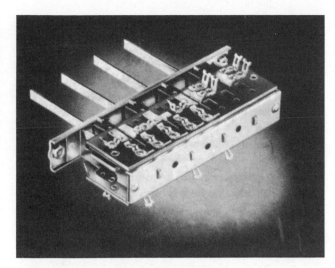

Push Button Switch.

same as for input switching. This switch permits each output line to be connected to any (or to none) of the program channels. When all buttons of the switch are in to OUT or disconnect position, a 620-ohm resistor (5 percent, ½-watt should be placed across the output line to prevent an increase in noise level.

OUTPUT LINES

Each output line comprises a bridging potentiometer, a bridging power amplifier, and a loudspeaker or group of loudspeakers.

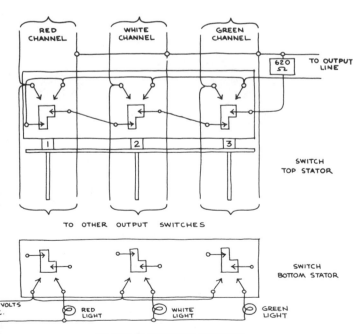

OUTPUT SWITCH WIRING

The bridging potentiometer provides output level control for each individual output and should be made in 20 steps of 2 dB per step. Again a vertical attenuator should be used. Its total resistance should be 25,000 ohms. This resistance permits as many as ten output lines to be switched onto the low-impedance program channel without audibility affecting its sound level.

Since the output lines are bridging lines having an impedance of approximately 25,000 ohms, they must be kept short. Capacitance in the interconnecting cables limits this length to 25 feet if a serious loss of high frequencies is to be avoided. If installation requires a greater length, stepdown transformers must be inserted closely adjacent to the output level control. United Transformer Company transformer LS-10X or HA-100X with reversed connections (a 10:1 stepdown ratio) is recommended for this use. This will result in a 600-ohm output line. Since the transformer supplies a bridging connection, a loss of 20 dB results unless a corresponding step-up transformer is used at the input of the power amplifier.

POWER AMPLIFIER

The power amplifier should be rack mounted, with low distortion, flat frequency response, and utilizing stabilized feedback. It should have a transformer-isolated high-impedance input of at least 25,000 ohms. Output power should be not less than 30 watts depending on the size of the auditorium and the requirements of the production. It must have sufficient gain to provide half its rated power output from an input of 1.228 volts. It is an advantage to have 5 to 10 dB more gain than needed if an internal gain adjustment is provided in each power amplifier. The following table shows minimum gain for each type of amplifier:

Output	Gain
30 watts	37.75 db
35 watts	38.50 db
50 watts	40.00 db
70 watts	41.50 db

Many of the available power amplifiers, otherwise well suited to the needs of a theatre sound-control system, are furnished without an input-isolating transformer. The reason for this is that these amplifiers are intended for less flexible installations, where switching occurs only between programs and therefore there is little need for precautions against noises caused by switching inputs.

In a theatre system switching must be silent. Strong precautions must be taken against switching pops, which for some perverse reason are, unless eliminated, loudest when switching is performed during a quiet scene. The use of an isolating input transformer is imperative.

When an isolating transformer is not included as part of the power amplifier, a suitable bridging transformer must be

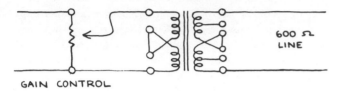

U.T.C. LS 10X OR HA 100X
CIRCUIT, STEPDOWN

600 Ω
LINE

GAIN CONTROL

Step-down transformer and Output Level Control.

installed. This transformer should be magnetically shielded to prevent hum pickup from adjacent equipment. When the line between the output control and the power amplifier is less than 25 feet, this isolating transformer can be a bridging type—that is, with a high-impedance primary. Where the power amplifier has sufficient gain, that is, at least 6 dB more than minimum gain, it is recommended that a 2:1 step-down transformer be used. United Transformer Company LS-20 (reversed) is recommended for this use.

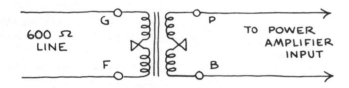

U.T.C. LS 20
BRIDGING CIRCUIT, STEP DOWN

600 Ω
LINE

G

F

P

B

TO POWER
AMPLIFIER
INPUT

Isolating Bridging Transformer.

Where power amplifiers must be so located that more than 25 feet of shielded, two-conductor cable must be used between output-level control and the power amplifier, a two-transformer step-down/step-up system is recommended. This system has been previously described under OUTPUT LINES. When this system is used, the same type of 10:1 transformer (United Transformer Company LS-104 or HA-100X) used for step-down at the output control is installed, in step-up connection,

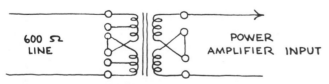

U.T.C. LS 10X OR HA 100X
CIRCUIT, STEP UP

600 Ω
LINE

POWER
AMPLIFIER INPUT

Step-up transformer circuit.

Output Control wiring for THE FOUNDERS.

in the power-amplifier input circuit and on the power-amplifier chassis.

On delivery, all power amplifiers must be checked for phase uniformity. Details of this check are included in Chapter X. Since it may be necessary to reverse output windings to keep all amplifiers in phase, an important specification for a power amplifier is that its output winding connections be reversible. This requirement eliminates those designs wherein the output windings are used as part of the inverse feedback circuit since such windings cannot be reversed.

Level Control.

POWER AMPLIFIER OUTPUT IMPEDANCES

When 100 feet or less of standard No. 16 AWG cable are used to connect the power amplifier to its associated loudspeaker, an output impedance of 16 ohms may be used with a power loss of less than 1 dB. However, when much longer lines are needed the copper cross section of the cable must be increased in proportion. It becomes economical to use higher output impedances which carry the same power at higher voltage but at lower current, thus permitting smaller copper cable cross sections. A practical limit to the impedance value (and so to the voltage) exists in usual electrical installation codes. These codes usually permit the use of rubber-covered cable without conduits or other armor if the transmitted signal does not exceed 70 volts.

Portable sound control console. At a station in the audience an operator may control inputs to balance direct and reproduced sound.

Broadcast and professional power amplifiers are equipped with output taps supplying this standard 70-volt output which corresponds to the following impedances

163 ohms on a 30-watt amplifier.
140 ohms on a 35-watt amplifier.
98 ohms on a 50-watt amplifier.
70 ohms on a 70-watt amplifier.
49 ohms on a 100-watt amplifier.

LOUDSPEAKERS

Loudspeaker selection should be based primarily on two characteristics: power handling capacity and a broad and uniform frequency response.

Unless the auditorium is extremely small, it is usually the best plan to use the loudspeaker having the largest power capacity, since loudspeakers, relatively speaking, are not very loud. The full output of the loudspeaker may rarely be used but the potential power must be provided. This is closely paralleled in the lighting department where most circuits are usually held on the dimmer.

It is generally advisable to allow for a larger power in the loudspeaker than that normally supplied by the power amplifier. The reason is that while overload of the amplifier results in distortion, overload of the loudspeaker may result in burnout or other physical damage. It is wise therefore to match a 35-watt amplifier with a loudspeaker capable of withstanding a constant electrical power of 35 watts and intermittent peaks of 50 watts. This proportion should be maintained for other power values.

If the selected loudspeaker does not reach these power requirements, it is advisable to use two rather than one loudspeaker in the enclosure.

FREQUENCY RESPONSE

A broad and uniform frequency response is especially necessary when non-musical sounds are to be reproduced. Frequency response must cover the whole range of human hearing. This requires the loudspeaker to reproduce a frequency range from 30 Hertz to at least 15,000 Hertz. To accomplish this it is usually necessary to use at least two loudspeakers—one for low-frequency and the other for high-frequency sounds. A crossover network prevents burnout of the high-frequency loudspeaker by the high-intensity low-frequency signals and filters the high frequencies out of the low-frequency loudspeaker circuit. This accomplishes two things: each loudspeaker is operated in the portion of the spectrum best suited to it, and frequency modulation of the high frequencies by the lows is avoided.

Frequency modulation in a loudspeaker is rarely evident in the moderate levels of the home sound system, but is an annoyance at the much higher levels used in the theatre.

As the intensity of low-frequency sound fields is increased, the cone or diaphragm of the loudspeaker must have increased amount of travel. If the amplitude of this travel becomes great enough, high frequencies generated by the same diaphragm will be frequency modulated by the low-frequency output of the loudspeaker. The pitch of the high-frequency sound will rise as the diaphragm moves toward the listener and will lower as the diaphragm moves away from the listener. The resulting frequency-modulated signal results in a form of distortion which is especially unpleasant to the pitch-sensitive ear.

ENCLOSURES

A loudspeaker is not by itself a complete item. Without its enclosure it behaves at low frequencies in very much the same manner as a pump without a gasket. To many persons, the term "loudspeaker" suggests a single mechanism, a paper or treated cloth cone attached to a coil of wire suspended in a magnetic field. The belief also exists that this unit may be purchased on its advertised reputation and then installed in a pretty cabinet—any cabinet, but preferably one containing a port for so-called bass reflex or other method of increasing the low-frequency range by resonating the cabinet. Adherence to this belief may provide fun for the faddist but it will not contribute to the control of sound.

The design and development of a resonated loudspeaker enclosure presents highly technical problems and should not be undertaken by the amateur. Even the professional must use a suitable laboratory and an anechoic sound chamber. Most of the cabinets designed and sold without a loudspeaker unit matched to it should be carefully avoided.

Many fine designs are available in which a resonated cabinet is designed and built by the loudspeaker manufacturer. In such cases the loudspeaker and cabinet are furnished together as a unit.

General purpose loudspeaker enclosure.

Care must be taken, however, to avoid any enclosure which results in a detectable acoustic resonance at low frequen-

cies since this resonance will remain no matter how the low frequencies are attenuated by filters in the amplifier circuits. A paradoxical situation results: a control system unable to exercise control over one portion of its spectrum.

Where the loudspeaker mechanism is purchased separately and a cabinet is to be built in the prop shop, it is recommended that a totally enclosed type of speaker cabinet be planned.

This type of enclosure should be rigidly constructed. The waterproof plywood used should be at least ¾ inch thick, and preferably 1¼ inches. Inside dimensions should be selected to avoid ratios such as 2, 3, and 4. Among possible dimensions are:

Depth a inches
Width 1.73 a
Height 2.46 a

Then the volume will be 4.25 a^3, in cubic inches.

Stand-mounted loudspeaker for voice dubbing.

The totally enclosed cabinet has the least effect on the characteristics of the loudspeaker. A correctly constructed enclosure affects only the natural resonance of the cone, as the smaller the volume the greater will be the increase in level of the resonant frequency. Therefore the enclosure should be as large as practicable. A rule-of-thumb standard generally applicable is

Outdoor weatherproof loudspeaker.

that the volume should never be less than .03 cubic feet per electrical watt rating of the power amplifier feeding the loudspeaker. The inner surface of the box should be lined with sound-absorbing material two inches thick. Hair felt, medium density glass fiber blanket or 4 lb/sq. ft. 2-inch thick glass fiber board or acoustical duct lining or absorbent cellulose material is satisfactory. If a grille cloth is used for covering the loudspeaker, it should be open mesh material, preferably plastic, so as to have no audible effect on the high-frequency response.

As an alternative to lining the cabinet an internal vane may be used. This is a section of flat board, at least one inch thick, of dense wood, placed diagonally in the cabinet from the top rear to bottom front and securely fastened. A clearance of about one inch is allowed on three of the sides and if necessary an opening may be cut to accommodate the rear of the loudspeaker mechanism.

The opening should clear the mechanism by about one inch. This vane will help to prevent resonance from *organ pipe* effect which occurs at frequencies whose wave length is once or twice that of the distance between opposite parallel surfaces of the enclosure.

Another kind of resonance is diaphragmatic resonance, wherein the wall of the cabinet, held at the edges and free in the center, vibrates as a drum head. A diagonal 3 x 1 batten screwed and glued to the inside (or outside) of each surface whose smallest dimension is greater than 12 inches, will reduce this sort of resonance. Although the diaphragmatic resonance is reduced below audibility, it may not be completely eliminated. Therefore, when castors or handles are to be attached to the enclosure, careful selection must be made to secure types which will not rattle. Solid handles are to be preferred to hinged handles and hung enclosures should not be equipped with

castors. When castored enclosures are placed on the stage floor, the weight of the loudspeaker and cabinet will usually prevent rattling.

It is strongly recommended that, if possible, one type of loudspeaker and one type and size of enclosure be decided upon and used throughout the control system. If loudspeakers having different acoustical balances are used, the *voice* of the sound will undergo a distracting change when moved from loudspeaker to loudspeaker.

SEVENTY-VOLT LINES AND TRANSFORMERS

Where 70-volt lines are used between the power amplifier output and the loudspeaker, a step-down transformer will be needed at the loudspeaker end of the line.

These transformers are rated according to the wattage rating of the power amplifier—a 35-watt transformer for a 35-watt amplifier, a 50-watt transformer for a 50-watt amplifier, and so on. One transformer is needed for each loudspeaker or group of loudspeakers.

If more than one loudspeaker is used in a single enclosure or if several loudspeakers, each in a separate cabinet, are used to terminate one power amplifier, only one output line and one 70-volt transformer will be needed. Matching the loudspeakers to the line is accomplished in the following manner: The nominal impedance of the loudspeaker in ohms (usually marked on the unit) should be divided by the number of loudspeakers to be connected to the transformer. The quotient will be the value of the impedance of the transformer-secondary winding to which the loudspeakers are to be connected in parallel. For example: two 16-ohm loudspeakers connect in parallel to the 8-ohm transformer winding. Three 16-ohm loudspeakers in parallel connect to the winding nearest in impedance to 5.3 ohms, usually the 4 or 6 ohm windings.

LOUDSPEAKER SWITCHING

Since each loudspeaker or group of loudspeakers has its associated power amplifier and since precautions against loudspeaker failure have been taken by providing for 40 percent greater power handling in the speaker than in the amplifier, it may be advisable to provide means for switching in case of amplifier failure. It is not necessary to interconnect all loudspeakers to all power amplifiers since a large and clumsy setup would result. It is not difficult, however, to equip each rack of power amplifiers with suitable switches.

One push-button switch assembly should be provided for each amplifier in the rack. It should have one button or condition for each loudspeaker. Since one loudspeaker or group is provided for each power amplifier, there should be as many buttons as there are amplifiers in the rack. Provision must be made to load each amplifier with a suitable dummy load when all contacts are disengaged, that is, when no buttons are depressed.

CHAPTER VIII

EQUIPMENT: INPUT SECTION AND CONTROLS

As is already apparent, the philosophy of design requires a basic reference as a starting point, in this case the VU meter. Design then proceeds in two directions, toward audience and toward source. Since the signal delivered to the audience is the reason for and the controlling factor in design, the output section has been treated first. This chapter carries equipment specification to the source.

LINE AMPLIFIERS

So far equipment has been dealt with from the reference point (Mixing Network and Volume Level Meter) through the power amplifier to the sink—the loudspeaker. It is now necessary to proceed in the other direction toward the various sources. These sources—microphone, phonograph, tape reproducer, electronic instrument—are generators of very low signals so that appropriate amplifiers and controls are needed.

First of these to be considered is the line amplifier. This is a fixed gain, moderately-low-power amplifier having a flat frequency response. It should have an undistorted output great enough to furnish the required power to the input of the mixing network. In the section on MIXING NETWORKS this peak power is shown to be plus 18 dBm for four input lines, or less, and plus 20 dBm for five or six input lines.

Input and output of each line amplifier must be isolated by an appropriate audio transformer coupling the unit to a 600-ohm input line and to a 600-ohm output line and mixing network. Since long, unshielded telephone lines are not part of the design of a theatre sound control system, there is no need for balanced interconnecting lines. Input and output transformer windings of the line amplifier must be connected for unbalanced use, that is, the center tap is not to be connected to ground. This permits the use of "T" attenuators instead of the more complicated, more expensive "H" attenuators.

For ease and convenience of installation and to provide interchangeability it is recommended that line amplifiers, mi-crophone amplifiers, rack mounting frames, and power supplies should all be the product of one manufacturer.

To simplify wiring and to eliminate the need for long interconnecting shielded cables, it is recommended that the line amplifiers and their appropriate power supplies be incorporated into the main control console which should also contain the input and output level controls, spectrum controls, channel switching, and level-indicating meters. Such a console is described in detail in the section on CONTROL PANELS.

INPUT LINES AND CONTROLS

The input to the line amplifier is the logical point for the insertion of input controls. Here the maximum input level remains constant in relation to the VU meter, at approximately 22 dBm. Provision must be made, in the form of a signal attenuator, to prevent this level from being exceeded. This point is also the suitable location for the insertion of spectrum controls or program equalizers.

To make this insertion possible, the line should be terminated by the installation of a suitable resistor across the 600-ohm input terminals of the line amplifier. A 5-percent, 1/2-watt, 620-ohm composition resistor is acceptable for this pur-

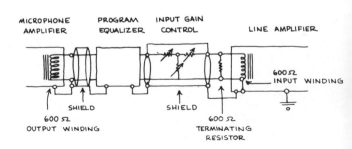

DETAIL OF INPUT CIRCUIT

pose. In the line ahead of the terminating resistor a 600-ohm attenuator must be inserted. Here again, as in the program line, a vertical attenuator is recommended. These attenuators must have zero insertion loss and twenty steps of 2 decibels loss per step.

REMOTE CONTROL

It has been previously recommended that, in addition to the sound booth, provision be made in certain circumstances for the control of the intensity level by an operator seated among the audience. This can be provided by the use of a small inconspicuous control box containing duplicates of the input level controls only, and held on the knees of the operator.

Back of Stevens sound control system, Mark II.

Cables from the main control console are at best permanently installed under the auditorium floor, ending in a single connector set into the floor and covered by a spring hinged lid. A short cable terminating in a companion connector leads to the remote control box. At the control console the cables connect into each input line immediately after the conventional input

level control. Provision must also be made for switching to allow the operator at the main console to cut the remote control in and out of the system.

SPECTRUM CONTROLS

At the point in the input line immediately preceding the input level control, filter networks should be inserted for the control of the frequency spectrum of each single input (Problems 8, 9, 10).

The purpose of such control is to produce a required dramatic effect and to provide hearing-contour compensation to restore natural balance when the needs of the production require sound levels greater or less than those of the original sounds.

A type of control available and technically suitable for insertion at this point, is the Program Equalizer. This is a constant-impedance T equalizer, permitting increase or decrease of low frequencies, decrease of the high frequencies and increase of the high frequencies with emphasis at 3000, 5000 or 10,000 cycles, as selected. It also contains a key for switching the whole control in or out of the circuit. Twelve decibels of increase and sixteen of decrease are available. Control is accomplished in fixed, calibrated steps permitting exact resetting of the chosen effect.

Insertion of the Program Equalizer in the input line causes a loss of fourteen decibels. For extreme effect two of these equalizers may be arranged in cascade, doubling the amount of equalization and, of course, the amount of insertion loss.

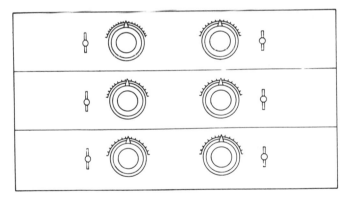

PROGRAM EQUALIZERS

Over-all spectrum control of the system is not recommended, as it entails insertion of the equalizer immediately after the VU meter. Since the resulting loss in gain will require compensation by additional amplifiers, there is no economy in over-all control. Furthermore, flexibility will be reduced since each input may require somewhat different equalization.

MICROPHONE AMPLIFIERS

In order to step up the extremely low power output of

microphones and similar devices, a microphone amplifier must be added to the circuit. This amplifier precedes the input level control and, when one is used, the Program Equalizer. Recommended low-level, low-impedance, professional microphones produce electrical output levels averaging −69 dBm. To increase the microphone power level to −22 dBm needed at the input control, a gain equal to the difference between these two levels is needed.

Therefore an amplifier having a fixed gain of 47 dB must be inserted into the circuit. It must have a flat frequency response between 30 and 15,000 cycles and an undistorted output of at least plus 4 dBm. It must contain input and output audio transformers to isolate input and output circuits. The output must be capable of operating into an unbalanced load of 600 ohms and the input must furnish proper termination to devices requiring 30/50 and 150 ohm loading. Output noise must not exceed −.72 dBm.

MICROPHONE FREQUENCY RESPONSE

The microphone, like the loudspeaker, is one of the weak links in the chain of sound reproduction equipment. Frequency responses in available models vary in quality from very poor to excellent. Although the best designs are usually expensive, price is not always an index.

It is strongly recommended, therefore, that the designer of a sound control system consider only those microphones whose makers furnish frequency response curves. Information on the effect of change in the angle of incidence on the response, or to put it more simply, the field pattern of the microphone's sensitivity at high frequencies should also be furnished. Frequencies from 30 to 15,000 cycles should be reproduced, with a minimum of peaks and valleys in the response. Many otherwise excellent microphones are characterized by a single broad peak. This is not too serious a fault, since such peaks can be equalized.

In broadcast and recording, it is usual to provide a flat frequency output by attenuating these peaks. This is generally done by the insertion of a suitable network immediately after the microphone amplifier.

MICROPHONE DIRECTIVITY

Directivity in microphones is an important factor in microphone selection. Here the pattern required depends upon the job to be done. Three directivity patterns are available—unidirectional, bi-directional, and non-directional. These patterns are shown in catalogues of manufacturers of professional grade microphones. Unidirectional patterns divide into three types:

(a) Cardioid microphones whose frequency sensitivity remains constant over an angle of at least 100 deg.
(b) Small-diaphragm condenser microphones whose frequency response remains constant over a very wide angle or kidney-shaped pattern.
(c) Supercardioid and long, phase delay, highly directive "shotgun" microphones.

Pattern (b) is extremely useful in the pickup of a symphony orchestra. It enables one microphone to replace several narrow-acceptance-pattern microphones and to maintain the effect of *ensemble* rather than the accentuation of separate instruments. Pattern (a) is more suitable than (b) and (c) for stereophonic pickup as its narrow pattern in the high frequencies provides a greater effect of *location*.

Bi-directional and non-directional patterns are useful in

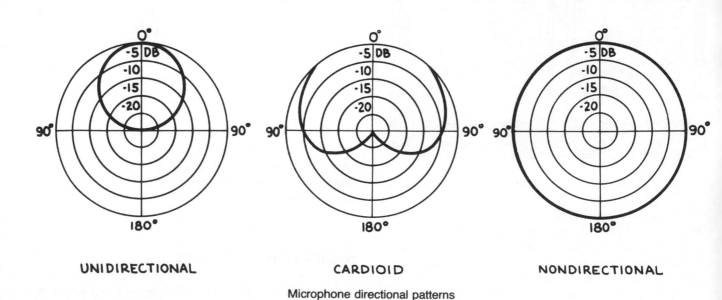

UNIDIRECTIONAL   CARDIOID   NONDIRECTIONAL

Microphone directional patterns

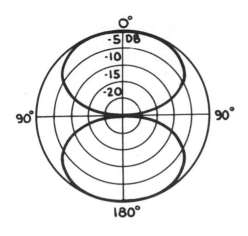

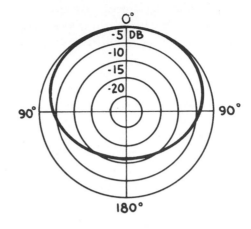

BIDIRECTIONAL

KIDNEY

Microphone directional patterns useful for special requirements.

microphones used for dialogue pickup since a number of actors can be grouped around them. Also, bi-directional and non-directional microphones pick up a much greater amount of reverberation than do those having unidirectional patterns. This characteristic must be taken into consideration when recordings are made for reproduction in reverberant theatre auditoriums.

MICROPHONE IMPEDANCE

High-impedance microphones are not recommended. In general, the quality obtainable from high-impedance microphones is not satisfactory for professional work. Even when the quality is reasonably good, the microphone must be operated within a few feet of the input amplifier, since the capacitance in more than six feet of cable will seriously reduce the high-frequency response.

In all of the high-quality professional microphones here considered, it is possible to adjust the output to an impedance of 30 or 50 ohms. Amplifier input circuits designed for 50-ohm source will accommodate a 30-ohm source without appreciable effect. Microphone impedances in the sound system should therefore be standardized in the 30- to 50-ohm range for uniformity and to permit the use of long cables.

MICROPHONE OUTPUT LEVEL

In manufacturers' catalogues, the electrical output of microphones is rated against a standard acoustical pressure of one newton per square meter. This pressure is also stated as an acoustic level of 94 dB and is about the level which results at a microphone diaphragm when the talker's mouth is within a few

inches. When used in reinforcement, microphones must operate at acoustical pressures of less than one newton per square meter. At 20 feet, a practical distance for dialogue pickup, any voice able to produce a pressure of one newton per square meter at the microphone should not need reinforcing.

Practical experience has shown that system gain requirements should be based on a sound source of not more than .25 newton per square meter. When needed gain is calculated, -12 dB should be added to the output shown in the catalogue for one N/m^2 pressure. If the output is given for a pressure of $0.1 \ N/m^2$ (1 dyne /cm^2), 8 dB should be added.

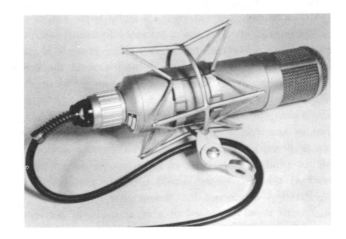

Elastic suspension of directional capacitor microphone.

When high-level microphones are used, a fixed T attenuator of 20 dB loss must be inserted between the microphone output and the microphone amplifier input to prevent overloading.

Note: Distortion appears in the frequency response of any microphone when it is placed too close to the talker's mouth. With some a rasping, spitting effect is heard, with others there is a booming exaggeration of the low frequencies. In velocity (ribbon) microphones this last effect is so pronounced that most of them are equipped with internal filters to attenuate low frequencies. It is therefore recommended that the microphone be placed at least three feet away from the sound source.

DISC REPRODUCTION

With simple and convenient magnetic recording readily available, facilities for disc recording are not needed as part of the theatre's sound control system. Hazards in disc operation make professional reliability difficult to attain. Operating in dim light under crowded conditions leads to the probability of error when selected sounds must accurately be extracted, on cue, from a number of discs, operating at different speeds. The precision and ease of operation of magnetic tape reproducers make this medium enormously preferable to disc reproduction.

Disc reproducers should be provided, however, for the purpose of dubbing from disc to tape, since large libraries of useful material are available on discs. Disc reproducers can be adapted to connect directly into the circuits of the tape recorder or may be connected into any of the input lines of the sound control system itself to facilitate selection of show material.

A manually operated turntable, *not a changer*, should be provided. The turntable should be of professional quality, dynamically balanced, and the platter itself should be fabricated of non-magnetic material. Four speeds are usually available—78, 45, 33-1/3, and 16-2/3 rpm. Very little recorded material is pressed on 45 or 16-2/3 rpm discs that is not also available on 33-1/3 rpm LP discs. Although 78 rpm discs, except for a few special items, are obsolete as far as high-quality music is concerned, some antique material useful in the theatre can be found on 78-rpm discs alone.

When selecting 78-rpm discs for use with high-quality reproducing equipment, it is imperative that shellac discs be rejected. The abrasive material used in shellac discs not only produces a high-level hissing background noise, but will rapidly grind away and seriously damage any reproducing stylus, *including the diamond*.

For precision work the plug-in type of magnetic pickup cartridge is preferable to the turnover type, as contributing less to the possibility of error.

For use with the two practical disc speeds, two types of stylus will be needed. For 78-rpm discs a stylus having a 3-mil radius will be required. For 33-1/3-rpm discs a stylus having a radius of 1 mil or less will be needed. In spite of advertised claims, there is no such thing as an all-purpose needle. Professional-quality magnetic pickup cartridges have shown uniform excellence in tests.

In modern recording, on disc or magnetic tape, the frequency response is pre-equalized to provide:

(a) The most efficient use of the medium.
(b) Maximum signal-to-noise ratio.
(c) Least overload distortion.

To ensure a flat frequency response a playback equalizer is needed. The frequency characteristics of this equalizer can be standardized since all present day high-quality discs are recorded to NAB standards (also known as RIAA). A passive equalizer conforming to these standards will suffice even in the playing of older, non-standard LP discs, since the deviation from standard is slight and can easily be compensated by the Program Equalizer. This passive equalizer should be designed to operate into a 50-ohm microphone input. Output level at this impedance should not exceed −55 dBm.

MAGNETIC TAPE RECORDING AND REPRODUCING

Magnetic recording equipment provides a most useful tool in the control of sound in the theatre. Records, faithful to the original sound, can be made using a microphone, or can be dubbed from disc or another tape. The linear form of the record makes editing a simple matter of selecting, cutting, and splicing. To best perform these functions requires professional equipment, having specified characteristics, as follows:

(a) A frequency response of 30 to 15,000 cycles with fixed NARTB equalization for 7.5 inch-per-second tape speed.
(b) Full width, single track.
(c) Monitoring from tape during recording.
(d) Reliable adjustment of head orientation.
(e) Normal recording level (zero on meter) at least 6 dB below 3 percent distortion level.
(f) VU meter level indication.
(g) Zero VU (+4 dBm), 600-ohm line output.
(h) Zero VU line bridging input plus a 50-ohm microphone input.

As in disc recording, tape recording frequency characteristics have been standardized to provide most efficient use of the medium and to achieve a maximum ratio of signal to noise. These standards have been adopted by the National Association of Broadcasters and are applied to the design of all professional-quality tape recorders. High-quality recorded tapes, both stereophonic and monophonic, comply with these standards.

Many tape recorder-reproducers, especially those of the

The Ampex ATR-700 tape recorder may be used for recording, editing, and production (Ampex Corp.).

Ampex model AG-440C tape recorder may be used for three-channel stereo (Ampex Corp.).

Portable magnetic recorder-producer, Nagra 4.2.

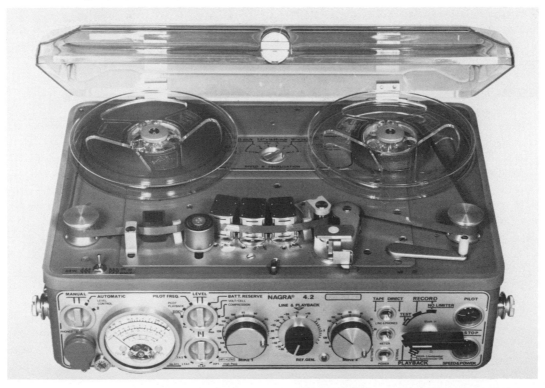

portable type, have excellent over-all frequency responses when playing their own recorded tapes. But when standard recorded tapes or tapes recorded on another type of instrument are reproduced, frequency response becomes an unknown quantity, and as such, no longer subject to control.

In order to have a maximum signal-to-noise ratio and to simplify the problems of editing and splicing, full-width single-track erase, record, and reproduce heads are required. These three heads, combined with suitable electronic circuits, enable the recording director to monitor tape output during recording. This is an important time-saving device, since it combines the recording session and listening session into one.

Serious high-frequency losses result when the magnetic gap, in either the record or reproduce head, becomes displaced a fraction of a degree from its normal position, perpendicular to the direction of tape travel.

In modern tape recorders, this position is adjustable and the gap angle may be aligned accurately with the aid of a specially recorded tape such as Ampex Standard Alignment Tape No. 01-31321-01 (for 7.5 inch per second tape speed).

Once the heads are aligned they must retain this orientation. In selecting a tape mechanism, examination of head mounting arrangements must be made to determine if the design is compatible with this requirement. If head supports are flimsy or if the head is easily moved about by light finger pressure, there will be good reason to suspect that head alignment will be difficult to maintain.

RECORDING LEVEL

A standard recording level must be maintained. A suitable recording level can be determined easily by checking the output of recorded tapes against the standard tape mentioned above. If the output is greater than from the standard tape, the recording level is too high. If the reverse is true, the recording level is too low.

Any system which merely shows a warning at the onset of distortion will not contribute to the making of good-quality recordings. In order to monitor recording level properly a device is needed which begins indication at least 20 dB below normal operating zero. The standard VU meter meets this requirement.

In order to keep all level controls at the operator's position, provision should be made in the design of tape reproducing circuits for 0 VU (+ 4 dBm) average maximum output into a 600-ohm line from tapes recorded at standard level. Tape reproducers meeting this requirement have no need for output level controls.

For the same reason that tape recording characteristics have been standardized, it is recommended that all tapes be recorded for flat reproduction. Equalization for dramatic effect will therefore be confined to the playback mode. Accordingly, the tape reproducer with its standard output of + 4 dBm is connected into the sound-control-system input line just ahead of the Program Equalizer. Maximum signal level at this point is −8 dBm. Therefore, a fixed 600-ohm T attenuator of 12 dB loss (the difference between + 4 and −8 dBm) should be inserted in the 600-ohm input line between the tape reproducer and the Program Equalizer.

In order to operate in record mode with other equipment of the sound control system, the tape recorder must have provision for an input which bridges a 600-ohm line at 0 VU level. To operate independently, a second input should accommodate a microphone requiring a termination of 30 to 50 ohms.

To permit dubbing from tape to tape and to provide for the copying of edited tape, it is necessary to have at least two tape recorders. One of these should be a standard studio model. The second, for convenience in the pickup of remote sounds, should be a portable model. Both of these recorder-reproducers must meet the eight requirements listed earlier in this chapter if compatibility with sound control objectives is to be maintained. Ampex Models AG440C and ATR700 are typical examples of the studio and portable recorders, respectively.

STEREOPHONIC RECORDING AND REPRODUCING

Stereophonic (commercial two-channel) recording is of minimal if any use in the theatre. Once recorded, the relationship between the two signals is fixed, allowing no further variation in designing the sound for the show. This does not derogate the use of authentic (three-or-more channel) stereophonic reinforcement.

Although two-track systems have been successfully developed for home use, three or more channels are needed to provide stereophonic effect over a wide stage. Studio equipment such as Ampex Recorder No. AG440C—4 can be furnished as stereophonic recorder-reproducers using three tracks.

OTHER SOURCES

All other sources should be equalized for a flat frequency output and should be equipped with an isolating output transformer. If the output level is greater than −8 dBm an output impedance of 600 ohms will be needed. If the output is less than −8 dBm, a 50 ohm output should be provided. A fixed-loss T network should follow. Its attenuation must be sufficient to reduce the output level to approximately −55 dBm.

CONTROL PANELS

Equipment for control and indication should be arranged for function and frequency of use. The design of the panel must minimize the possibility of operator error and allow for rapid operation. Controls must operate in a natural manner, based on human articulation and muscular capacity, and in a direction compatible with that of the desired result. Progress from OFF to ON and from LOW to HIGH level should be in an upward direction, and input to output progress from left to right. Controls most often handled should be placed nearest the

operator on a slanted panel. Infrequently adjusted controls are best located above often-handled controls and in such a manner that their condition is readily apparent. Meters and other indicators belong at eye level. Luminous color-coded indicators which glow but do not radiate light accompany each action.

It is recommended that control panels be mounted at an angle of 30 to 45 degrees from the horizontal, in three or four sections arranged about the operator, so that he may easily reach any control. At the base of each panel a small horizontal shelf will allow the operator to steady his forearm to reduce fatigue and to contribute toward smooth manual control. The shelf should be located at standard table height, 30 inches above the floor, for the convenience of a seated operator. A typical arrangement of controls and indicators is shown in the illustration titled Control Panels.

In the control panels, those at the operator's left contain input-circuit intensity and spectrum controls; the center panel contains channel masters and VU meters. Output controls are placed to the operator's right.

Closely associated controls and indicators are placed together in vertical arrays, which serve equally for input or output circuits. Color-coded channel push buttons are at the bottom. Above them is the vertical gain control. Immediately above the gain control is a row of channel-indicating lights, colored

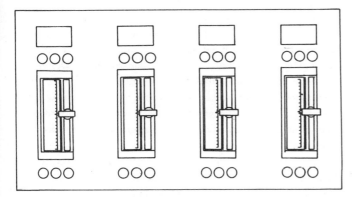

INPUT CONTROLS

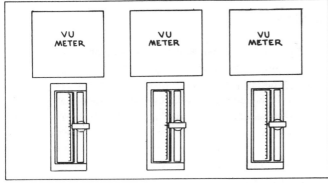

CHANNEL MASTER CONTROLS

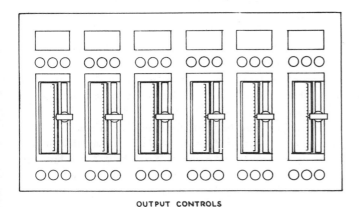

OUTPUT CONTROLS

Control Panels.

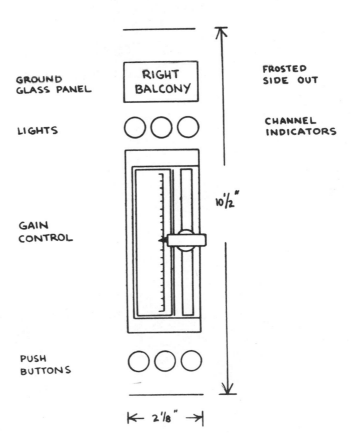

DETAIL OF CONTROL PANEL.

according to the channel code. At the top of the array is an illuminated ground glass window with the frosted side out to permit pencilled identification. Illumination of the window must be kept low to prevent light spills during blackouts. For the same reason, frosted rather than faceted lenses should be used in the channel indicating lights. Very small lenses and lens holders are available.

PHYSICAL ASSEMBLY

In order to keep interconnecting cables as short as possible, line and microphone amplifiers, with their associated power supplies, should be installed in the consoles which support the control panels. These amplifiers, on plug-in chassis, must be readily accessible from the front, for ease of testing and replacement. All connections are made at the rear of the consoles.

Microphones and line amplifiers should be installed near associated controls, in the left console. Power supplies should

Sound control system for the Provincial Halls, Calgary and Edmonton, Alberta. Separate sections provide for all dramatic requirements, public address, and monitoring for communications and acoustic envelope.

be installed in the right console. Telephone equipment and other cueing-signal apparatus can be put into the center console. Crowding must be avoided. If sufficient space between units and large openings at bottom and top of consoles are provided, it will not be necessary to use blowers. Natural-air-current ventilation, based on the rise of heated air, is preferred to forced ventilation, since blowers generate noise.

Commercially available control panels are made for recording and broadcast use and are *not* suitable for theatre sound control. They generally lack the color and pilot light coding required by the low illumination in the control booth. Designed for multi-microphone mixdown to two channel stereo, they cannot meet the operational needs of the theatre. Controls are often too small or inconveniently placed for theatre operation. Custom-made consoles using components here described are not inordinately expensive.

Power amplifiers, if mounted in relay racks, according to the manufacturer's installation directions, will not require forced ventilation. These racks can be located behind the operator. Here again crowding must be avoided. Clear floor space both before and behind the racks will facilitate inspection and maintenance.

CABLES

Interconnecting cables should be hung overhead or run in channels under the floor. A single rule applies to all signal wiring, whether within the consoles or connecting consoles to racks. Telephone practice must be followed, a pair of conductors must be used for each signal loop. Cable shields must never be used as signal conductors. No common conductor can be tolerated since cross talk will result. All shielded cable must be insulated and protected by a tough rubber covering on all cables for external use.

Color coded, twisted pair, stranded AWG No. 20 can be used on the rear of the control panels to connect program channel switches and controls which operate at 0 VU level. Input circuits to line and microphone amplifiers must be shielded.

Standard stage cable, with two conductors not smaller than AWG No. 16, can be used to carry power from the electric mains and to connect power amplifiers to loudspeakers. All low-level signal lines must be standard two-conductor, shielded microphone cables. In order to fit suitable connectors properly, 9/64-inch over-all diameter cabling (min. 0.235 inch, max. 0.290 inch) should be used. Examples are: Alpha No. 1250 which has an over-all diameter of 0.270 inches; Belden No. 8412, 0.263 inches; and Birnbach No. 772, 0.280 inches. The conducting wire size in all of these is AWG No. 20.

Ground leads should never be soldered to braided shields, as this practice results in charred and weakened insulation. Instead, the braided shield should be unraveled, strand by strand, with the aid of a smooth, sharp pointed awl or machin-

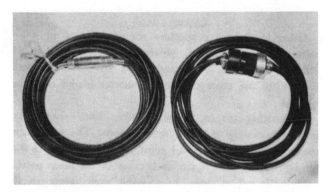

Typical Cable assemblies, in 25-foot coils. Left, microphone; right, Loudspeaker.

Connectors: upper, Cannon type for microphone cables; lower, Hubbell Twistlock types for Loudspeaker cables.

ists' scriber. The unraveled strands can then be twisted into a "pigtail" which can be soldered into the connector terminal.

CONNECTORS

It is strongly recommended that a different type of connector be used for each function. For instance, three-conductor microphone connectors such as Cannon XL-3 should be used for low-impedance low-level circuits. Four-conductor connectors such as Cannon XL-4 can be used for higher-level 600-ohm lines. In such connectors it is standard practice to solder the white insulated signal wire to terminal 3 and the black wire to terminal 2. Shield is connected to terminal 1. When four terminal connectors such as XL-4 are used, the cable shield is unbraided and twisted into two pigtails, one of which solders to

terminal 1, the other to terminal 4. To maintain phase relationships, this matching of color coded conductors to certain terminals must be standard throughout the system.

Other distinctive connectors should be used in loudspeaker circuits. Armored, polarized connectors such as Hubbell Nos. 7690, 7693 and 7699 are recommended, especially for use onstage where connector blades must be protected.

Alternating-current, 60-cycle power lines should be wired permanently into the sound booth. The main line must be fused separately and must be independent of the stage lighting system. A circuit breaker in the main power lead is preferred to fuses. In addition, each power amplifier and power supply must be individually fused. Current capacity of each fuse should be no greater than that needed to supply normal current to the unit. An overlarge fuse is no protection.

Close adherence to the practice of using a different type of connector for each function will prevent disastrous mistakes such as the plugging of loudspeaker voice-coil circuits into A.C. power lines.

In contrast to the electric wiring code, in which hot lines always terminate in protected female connectors, and exposed terminal male connectors are used only at the load, it is standard practice in sound systems to use female connectors at the input of amplifiers and male connectors at the output of all except power amplifiers. The reason for the practice is this: Sensitive input circuits must be protected against contact with ground or the human body. Such contact usually results in noises which are more distracting to an audience than the onstage stroll of the theatre cat during a love scene.

TEST EQUIPMENT

One Audio oscillator 20 to 20,000 Hz.
Two electronic voltmeters, 1 millivolt to 100 volts rms.
One Voltohmeter.
Two fixed potentiometers, broadcast quality.
Dummy loads for loudspeaker voice-coil lines:
    One 8-ohm, 100-watt wire-wound resistor or
    One 16-ohm, 100-watt wire-wound resistor.
Dummy loads for 70-volt lines:
    One 160-ohm 100-watt wire-wound resistor for 30-watt amplifiers or
    140-ohm, 100-watt wire-wound resistor for 35-watt amplifiers or
    100-ohm 100-watt wire-wound resistor for 50-watt amplifiers or
    70-ohm 100-watt wire-wound resistor for 70-watt amplifiers or
    50-ohm 225-watt wire-wound resistor for 100-watt amplifiers.
One Dummy microphone consisting of a 33-ohm ½-watt 5 percent resistor connected between terminals 2 and 3 of Cannon Connector XL-3-12.

STANDBY EQUIPMENT AND SPARE PARTS

At least one power amplifier, one line amplifier, one microphone amplifier, and a suitable power supply in addition to those making up the system, should be installed as standby equipment. The extra power amplifier is fitted with all needed connectors and installed with the others in the relay racks to be readily available when needed.

The microphone amplifier, the line amplitier, and the power supply, all plug-in units, can be stored in a suitable space in the console for substitution if the pre-performance check discloses a defective unit.

Fuses are most critical items. Therefore the stock of replacement fuses must never be less than the total quantity of each type used in the system. A stock of small replacement parts is not needed. It is advised instead that defective units be returned to the manufacturer.

CHAPTER IX

ORGANIZATION AND PLANNING

SOUND CONTROL is a part of the planning of every production. How the line will be spoken and from where, the balance of the orchestra, the dynamics of the aria must be established. The planning of electronic control is no less important and should begin as soon as any other element of planning.

RESPONSIBILITY: SOUND DESIGNER

The sound designer develops the sound plan from the script and the director's requirements, plans and supervises the installation, operation and maintenance of sound equipment for the production, directs the making of special recordings and integrates the sound planning, assembly and rehearsal with the director, musical director and the technical departments.

Unfortunately, the need for the sound designer is too little understood at the time of this writing. Planning of sound control is often done by the stage manager and the contractor who supplies the electronic equipment or the technician who operates it. This may be satisfactory if the use of electronically reproduced sound is confined to producing effects, for here the sound technician is merely the logical successor to the property man who traditionally makes the off-stage effect sounds.

In many productions, the planning progresses a considerable distance without the responsibility for developing the sound being definitely assigned. Scenery and lights are the designer's responsibility, but the stage manager often gets the responsibility for the sound by default. The stage manager has enough to do without this added duty. Moreover, he is seldom an engineer and is caught between the expressed requirements of the director and the limitations of equipment which he too often does not understand.

His task is not helped by the fact that the language of sound is often confusing to people of the theatre. The technical language necessary to describe electronic equipment and auditory phenomena precisely is not generally understood in the theatre nor is adequate use made of the more generally familiar

musical terminology which can be applied with considerable success to the problem of conveying ideas from one person to another in the field of sound. Much time is lost in planning and

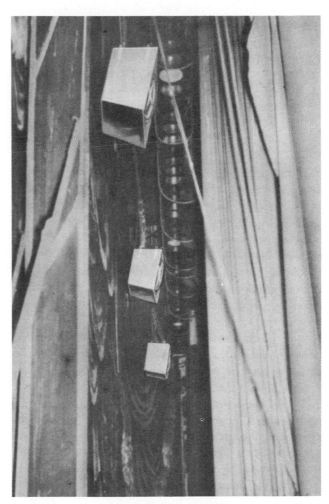

Loudspeakers flown backstage, old Metropolitan Opera House.

more in setup and operation because the showman too seldom knows how to express his requirements in technical terms, and the engineer or technician may have difficulty in satisfying needs otherwise stated. If the production depends upon electronic control of sound for essential or highly significant elements requiring scope or subtlety, the sound designer is essential. He must also plan the equipment, supervise its assembly and testing, develop the setup sheet and cue sheets, and supervise the operation in technical and cast rehearsals and in as many performances as are necessary to achieve smooth operation.

For productions playing in houses not adequately equipped, the sound equipment is supplied by an independent concern which operates just as does any dealer in stage lighting equipment. According to the rules of I.A.T.S.E., the sound technician who actually installs and operates the equipment is a member of the electrical department, though in case of a heavy show he may rate as a department head. The supplier of equipment maintains it both in New York and on the road.

In a permanently staffed, academic or community theatre, the technical director may serve as the sound designer. Where a permanently installed sound control system is available and adequate, as it is in a few non-commercial houses, setup, operation and maintenance are usually handled by house personnel.

For purposes of the following discussion, it will be assumed that there is a sound designer, responsible for sound control, though this function may in fact be delegated to a consultant, the stage manager, the sound technician, or any other handy member of the producing organization.

ORIGIN OF THE PLAN

The treatment of sound may be prescribed in the script, or it may be a modification or amplification—suggested by the director, star, or composer—of the concept expressed in the script. Often it is the combined effort of several of these. The concept of the use of sound in the LIVING NEWSPAPER was largely Elmer Rice's. Sidney Howard's last completed script, MADAM, WILL YOU WALK, was quite specific in its sound requirements. Helen Hayes, producing Barrie's MARY ROSE for ANTA, developed the sound plan with the director. As cited in Chapter V, notable sound control plans for the works of Shakespeare, O'Neill and Wagner have been developed by Margaret Webster, Cheryl Crawford, Herbert Graf and Erwin Piscator.

DIRECTOR

The sound designer obtains from the director of the production an indication of style, mood, and tempo of the production and specific indications as to the end results he wants; i.e., the apparent direction, movement, dynamics, and other special characteristics of sound. The director will also prescribe the operational requirements that apply to the whole show such as time limits within which shifts must be accomplished.

COMPOSER, CONDUCTOR

In the case of a musical, the composer or conductor or both will supply information as to the size and preferred location for the orchestra. With composer, conductor, and director, the sound designer will work out the requirements for musical bridges and cues, and the movement, spatial quality, or other element which must be provided electronically. Kurt Weill made excellent use of electronic sound control, as had, more recently, Richard Rodgers and Robert Russell Bennett.

DESIGNER

From the designer's ground plans, elevations, and working drawings, the technical director can determine how scenery will affect sound. He will be able to plan upstage loudspeaker and microphone pickup positions and hanging positions for microphone enclosures. Where loudspeakers must be built into scenery, the necessary toggles must be inserted and cuts made. The effect of the scenic materials on the transmission or reflection of sound can be calculated and the necessary electronic compensation planned. Often where transmission or projection of sound seems indicated, reflection can be substituted, and the handling of the show thereby simplified. This was the case in Elmer Rice's TWO ON AN ISLAND, a very heavy show in which Jo Mielziner's sets were designed to accommodate the loudspeakers, and the sound was reflected from the stage floor.

STAGE MANAGER

With the stage manager, the sound designer can work out the location and cueing requirements for orchestra, onstage and backstage choruses, electronic and prop sound sources, and positions for all equipment onstage, backstage, in the pit, and in the house.

With the information so far in hand the technical director can plan his electronic sound control equipment and send a block diagram specification and schedule of equipment to the supplier, or if the theatre is adequately equipped, specify the basic setup to his sound technician.

INTEGRATION OF SOUND AND OTHER PRODUCTION ELEMENTS

Developing of the sound control plan, designing of the system, procuring and testing of equipment and integrating it into the operation of the show take a long time. Even if there is a permanently installed sound control system in the theatre, *sound will take almost as long to prepare as any other element of production*. It is therefore essential that commitments be made as soon as possible in all departments having a bearing on the sound. Many can be made at the first production meeting.

For voices which must be dubbed, the sound designer will have to schedule recording sessions when the actors are available. He will have to arrange to test all his sounds for character, origin and movement, to satisfy the director. He will have to test and get approval of all his sequences which use live pickup. All this scheduling means having the equipment set and tested early, the players and singers available and the theatre quiet. This last requirement is often the hardest to handle. No department ever has the theatre all to itself long enough, if we are to believe the department heads.

ACOUSTICAL CONDITIONS OF THE THEATRE

The technical director will observe and measure, where necessary, the acoustical conditions of the theatre and calculate the extent to which these are modified by the scenery. He will apply these data to his plan for the type and position of loudspeakers. For example: (a) If the house has sound absorbent material in any considerable quantity on walls or ceiling, the surfaces thus treated are useless for reflection of sound. Sound which should appear to come from above or around the audience or via walls and ceiling from an unidentifiable source, must be directly projected. (b) If the stage house is highly reverberant and the fly loft not filled with flown scenery, and projection from backstage or upstage of the scenery is to be undertaken, highly directional loudspeakers must be employed to keep the sound from getting loose in the fly loft and picking up reverberation unless that is specifically desired.

In a live house the audience will absorb enough sound to require 6 to 12 dB higher level for all sound when the house is full than when it is empty.

The orchestra pit is often an inefficient sound source location and may require selective as well as general reinforcement. Too often the sound designer is expected not only to direct, supplement, extend, and enhance the sound in the show, but at the same time to correct the acoustical deficiencies of the theatre.

OPERATING POSITION

Operating positions for sound control are usually difficult to find if the theatre is old and not planned for sound control. The ideal operating position is a seat in the audience area. Next best, and required in any modern theatre as equipment location as well as for operation, is a booth at one side of the projection booth with the face completely open. In old theatres a control booth can sometimes be built of scenic materials by the carpenter and occupy the space of about 6 or 8 seats at the back of the balcony. The management, with an eye on the box office, will complain about this. The Ritz Theatre in New York had an unoccupied stub gallery above the balcony where there was plenty of room for all sound control equipment and where the operator could see and hear as well as most of the audience.

Operation from boxes is sometimes undertaken as a compromise. If the management will stand for the price of two operators, control may be split with setup undertaken at the control console backstage or in the trap room, and operation by remote console which the operator can hold on his lap in a seat out front. This sort of operation is quite satisfactory except where movement of the sound is required in which case operation of both input and output sections of the console from out front is required. In the Juilliard production of the opera THE MOTHER, the sound control system was operated by the conductor from a remote console beside his desk in the pit. A basic principle which, if violated, makes consistently good performances impossible, is: *the operator must be so located that he sees and hears the show as the audience does.*

EQUIPMENT ONSTAGE

Equipment onstage must be integrated into the plan for the use of stage space, the hanging plan, and the shifts. Such equipment includes loudspeakers mounted in openings in a false proscenium as in the LIVING NEWSPAPER, or loudspeakers set in flats as in TWO ON AN ISLAND. Loudspeakers on the stage floor behind the scenery must be mounted on dollies. When scenic materials are in front of the loudspeakers, the absorption must be calculated (Chapter III) and compensated.

In MADAM, WILL YOU WALK, it was necessary to project live speech from a very restricted area upstage. Satisfying this need required cutting the back wall of the set and concealing the opening with a table and a vase of flowers.

It is a good rule to build loudspeakers into the scenery and properties as often as possible. Such an arrangement guarantees their playing position and orientation, simplifies shift, and reduces the number of men necessary onstage. The alternative of putting loudspeakers on stands or dollies and handling them at each shift is time-consuming and hazardous. For speech in

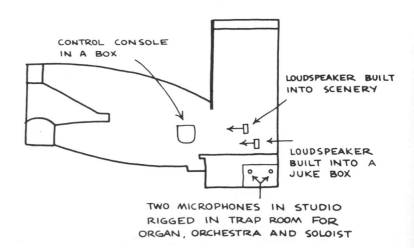

Equipment layout for HAPPY BIRTHDAY.

perspective as in the case of Bottom or the Ghost in HAMLET, only a 2-inch loudspeaker unit is necessary and such units can be very easily concealed in almost any set piece or prop.

Backstage control for electronic effects requires placing the equipment where the operator can take cues easily, preferably from the lines or business.

FLOWN EQUIPMENT

It is axiomatic that all equipment that can be taken off the floor should be kept off the floor. When loudspeakers can be flown, even though they work on the floor, it is wise to fly them. This prevents errors in setup, keeps cables off the floor, and makes it unnecessary to disconnect units when they are struck. Hanging positions which are often found useful are: three loudspeakers on a batten, upstage in *four*, one center, and the two at the extreme ends of the batten; three loudspeakers flown in *one*, just upstage of the first electric, and occasionally a group of three, as already indicated, built into a false proscenium. This last is the best mounting position for stereophonic reinforcement of stage speech.

Microphones are best flown for most onstage pickup positions except the footlights. The hung microphone has the great advantage that it is immune to floor rumble. Sports arenas use this system for the announcer's microphones; nightclubs can avoid noise and distortion by flying the microphone out of the performer's reach. Mayor LaGuardia was an inveterate microphone nuzzler, with the result that nobody could understand the words. The engineer (Mallory) who set up for his speeches gave him a dummy microphone to caress and picked him up from a hanging microphone. The results were excellent.

Microphones in enclosures must in most cases be hung on spot lines where the performer using the microphone can see and hear the stage, and where they can be taken out when they are not working.

When choruses must be accommodated backstage, space must be provided for them and kept clear of scenery and props. For such installations it is desirable to have a microphone hung permanently. Backstage orchestras and choruses, located onstage or in the trap room, will have to be isolated from backstage noise, usually by draperies. Such enclosures are non-reverberant. Music played or sung in a live dressing room often sounds better.

Sound sources must be kept away from stage machinery which makes a noise or from any location where local noise might interfere with pickup.

DEPARTMENT HEADS' PLANNING

The carpenter, chief electrician, and sound technician are all concerned with the location of electronic equipment. The carpenter may have to build dollies to mount the equipment backstage, or screens to conceal it in the balcony, or he may have to keep certain spaces clear for moving set pieces. The electrician has to plan the location of cables with consideration of the fact that low-level pickup lines cannot parallel A.C. lines without picking up hum. He must also supply a source of 117-volt A.C. power. In the Shubert Theatre in New Haven the A.C. main has a limited capacity and supplies the marquee

SET-UP SHEET FOR DEMONSTRATION OF SOUND CONTROL IN SCENES FOR

Cue No.	Scene No.	Scene Description	Time	Warning	Cue	Sound	Source	Input No.			Input Control Setting			Inp
1		Overture	00:00	Stage Manager	Stage Manager	Orch	Pit	4	5	6	18	16	16	
2		Voice		Stage Manager	Stage Manager	Voice	Tent Mike	1						
		Voice												
a		Voice		Stage Manager	Stage Manager	Voice	Tent Mic	1						
b		Voice				Voice	Tent Mic	1						
c		Voice				Voice	Tent Mic	1						
d		Voice				Voice	Tent Mic							
2 f		Intro Music		Voice line	Ok-Charlie	Orch.	Pit	4	5	6				
3	1	Macbeth		Stage. Mgr.	Curtain Starts	Thunder	Thunder Screen		1					

lights. During rehearsals the sound system works well. When the marquee lights are turned on the voltage drop is so great that the system becomes inoperative. Several openings have done without sound because the electrician did not provide for this contingency.

PROP SOUND

When prop sound effects are employed, their location is critical and they must be tried out for position and accepted by the director if they are to be used without electronic control. If the prop sound is to be electronically reproduced, the location of the prop devices will be governed by consideration of pickup and cueing. Any effect that an electronic sound system can transmit can be recorded and reproduced. It is therefore safest and wisest to use tape records for all such effects.

PROCEDURE

After the sound designer has developed his sound score from the script and the requirements of composer and designer, he confirms and modifies it by sitting in at enough rehearsals to discover precisely what is intended. At such times he can settle with the director points which have not been defined up to that time.

The sound technician who will operate the system will also start to make a sound setup sheet which contains all the information necessary to set up an operation.

Control settings are filled in at rehearsal, corrected and modified at preview. The term stereo refers to a multi-channel output manually controlled for movement. Ferranti refers to a nine-octave attenuator. Spotter refers to a transcription cueing device.

MAGNETIC RECORDING

Any direct source of recorded sound other than magnetic tape is now obsolete for theatrical use. By getting rid of disc records, the production is ensured against deterioration of the recorded signal. Cueing is no longer a problem and there is no chance of groove skipping, or of playing discs out of order or wrong side up.

In magnetic recording, the excellence of the result depends much more upon the quality of the recording equipment than upon the skill of the operator. Almost exact reproduction is possible and several re-recordings can be made without introducing audible distortion or noise if professional equipment is used.

A certain amount of technical ability and knowledge of the art is required. This ability and knowledge can be developed by a reasonable amount of study and practice, especially in the mechanical aspects of recording. No longer is it necessary to spend many years gaining experience and discipline in order to make good recordings as was required in the cutting and processing of discs.

It is not within the province of this book to cover the history and technical aspects of magnetic recording. The recording director and operator can, nevertheless, profit from some background study of the subject.

WHICH TRADITIONAL MECHANICAL CONTROL OF SOUND IS INADEQUATE

Output No.	Output Channel Color			Output Control Setting			Speaker Plug			Panel Jack			Speaker Location	Operating Technique
	1	2	3										Stereo Speakers	
2 3	R	W	G	16	16	16	1 2	3 7 8	A	B F G	C		1 2 3 Expos, W.H., E.H. Balcony	
5		W					2 4 5	6	B	H I J				
4 5 6		W		Change up/Down			2 4 5	6	B	H I J				
	G	W					2	6	B	J				
7		W					7			F			Pocket	take out middle on Ferranti
														At end of voice change input 1 to drum & compensate
2 3 4 5		W					1 2 4	3 5	A	B H I	C			at end of orch. shift speaker plugs 1,2,3 to Backstage Overhead roll & fade out on laughter

Cue #	Scene No	Scene Description	Time	Warning	Cue	Sound	Source	Input No.	Input Control Setting	Input Co
3a	1	Macbeth			{ segue	Prokofiev	WETT	2		G
4					{ segue	Witches	Spotter D-1	3	16	
5				wierd sisters	-- charms wound up	witches				
6				inhabitants 'o the earth	-that you are so - speak	witches	Spotter D-1			
7				thane of Cawdor	-- be king hereafter	witches				
8				seeds of time	neither beg nor fear	witches	Spotter 6-A2-98			
9a					Banquo and Macbeth- all hail	Thunder Witches	Screen D-1			stri
10				let us speak	-till then, enough. Come.	Orch.	Pit	4 5 6	16 16 16	4 R
11					segue	Voice	Booth	1	16	W
12						Orch.	Pit	4 5 6	16 16 16	4 R
13	II	Tempest		Beginning of Overture	Opening of Curtain	Ariel	Tent	1		
14				that's my noble master	go, hence with diligence	Orch.	Pit	4 5 6	16 16 16	4 R
15				Keep a good tongue	shall not suffer indignity	Whistle Cut1	Spotter D2	3		3
16				I am subject to	of the island	Ariel	Tent	1		
17					thought is free	Tabor & Pipe	spotter D2	3		3
18										
19				forgive me my sins	I defy thee	Thunder	Thunder Screen	2		2
20				Lead monster	I'll follow, Stephano	Orch.	Pit			2
21				let it be tonight	tonight: no more / Segue	Thunder Ariel	Spotter D-2	2 3		3
22					you and your ways	Prospero	Booth	1		1
23					Follow, I pray you	Orch.	Pit	4 5 6	16 16 16	4 R
24					End of Orchestra	Voice	Booth	1		1
25	III	Dream		Voice Line	o.k. charlie	orch	Pit	4 5 6		4 R
26				Sing me now asleep	then to your offices	Fairies	Spotter D-3	3		
27				Segue	end of music	Fairies	Spotter D-3	3		
28				your cue is past-it is never tire	as true as truest horse	Bottom	Spotter D-4	3		
29				doth more me	I love thee	Bottom				
30				segue	I have enough to serve mine own turn	Bottom				
31				weeps every little flower	enforced chastity	Bray				
32				thy sleek, smooth head	my gentle joy	Bottom				
33				to say what dream it was	me thought I was	Bray				
34				Segue	sing it at her death	Orch.	Pit	4 5 6		R
35				Segue	End of overture	Voice	Booth	1		
34		Tocatta					Western Elec. D-5	2		W
		Intermission								
40		Overture		Stage Mgr.	Stage Mgr.	Orch	Pit	4 5 6		4 R
41	V	Janes		Segue	End. of orch.	Drum	Drum	2		

ut No.	Output Channel Color	Output Control Setting	Speaker Plug	Panel Jack	Speaker Location	Operating Technique
					Overhead Speakers	Background music Fade with Banquo & Macbeth
2 3	G		1 2 3	L M N		
7 8	R	28 28 28	6 7 8	E F G	Stand Speakers	
						lift spotter
						set spotter on
						lift spotter
						put spotter on
						1 ft. spotter, strike disc #1,
					Procen-R Expo Procen-L	at end of witches shift drum to input #2, booth mike to input #1
2 3	R W G	16 16 16	1 2 3	A B C		Backstage overhead to proscenium
5 6	W		2 4 5 6	B H I J		Inputs 4,5,6 green to stereo setup.
2 3	R W G	16 16 16	1 2 3	A B C	Procen-R Expo Procen-L	
						shift output to pit
4, 5, 6, 7	W		2 4 5 6 7	B H I J D		End of orchestra shift prosc. to backstage overhead
2 3	R W G		1 2 3	A B C		
4 5 6 7	W		2 4 5 6 7	B H I J D		Put spotter on
1 3			1 3	E - G		Lift spotter
5 6 7 8	3		2 4 5 6 7 8	B H I J M N		add speakers for thunder
4 5	W		2 4 5	B H I		up on 8th bar & out
4 5	W		4 5	H I		Thunder on word cues
4 5 6 7 8	W		2 4 5 6 7 8	B H I J M N		
2 3	R W G		1 2 3	A B C		
4 5 6	W		2 4 5 6	B H I J		Hook up & set stage witch speakers
2 3	R W G		1 2 3	A B C		
7 8	R		6 7 8	L M N	OHSR OHSC OHSL	Fade up Fairies - spot to be sure to get first note
7 8	R		6 7 8	L M N		End Disc at end of music - Strike disc & put on Ass disc
7 8	R		6 7 8	E F G	Stage Stand Speaker	Drop Spotter — Follow Bottom with Speakers
						Drop Spotter
						Lift Spotter
						Spot
						Spot - Run to end of cut
					Center Stand	Spot - strike disc
2 3	R W G		1 2 3	A B C		
4 5 6	W		2 4 5 6	B H I J	Exp. WH EH Bal.	
	W		1 2 3 4 5 6 7 8	A B C L N I J L M N	PR Exp PL WH EH Bal OHSR OHSL	

Intermission shift

			1 2 3 4 5 6 7 8	A B C L N H I K		
2 3	R W G	16 16 16	1 2 3	A B C	Procenium Rt. Cen. Lt.	Start drum on last note orchestra - inaud.
6 7 8	W		8	K	Floor	

Cue #	Scene No.	Scene Description	Time	Warning	Cue	Sound	Source	Input No.	Input Control Setting	In,
42		Jones			you kin bet yo Boy is you gone crazy mad	Drum	Drum	2		
43				lights match		Formless Fears	Spotter D-3	3		
44				pistol shot	git in	isdrum beats	Drum	2		
45				Segue	13th Beat	Orch	Pit	4 5 6		R
46						Voice				
47	VI	Lazarus		Segue	Voice	Chant	Spotter D-7	3		
48				Segue	Segue	Crowd	Spotter D-7	3		
49				Segue	2nd.- Ha - ha-ha-ha	Crowd	Spotter D-7	3		
50					Lazarus!	Crowd	Spotter D-7	3		
51a				Segue	for men on earth	Crowd	Spotter D-7	3		
52										
53				Segue	there is no death for man	Lazarus	Western Elec. D-8	2		
54				Stop his laughter	We love his laughter	Crowd	Spotter D-7	3		
55				Segue	the fire calls me	Crowd	Spotter D-7	3		
55				in the name of man's solitude { Tiberius	What is beyond there, Laz.	Crowd	Spotter D-7	3		
56						Laz. laughter	Western Elec. D-8	2		
57				Life, Eternity, Stars, Dust. God's Eter. Laughter		Laz. Laughter	Western Elec. D-8	2		
58				you make him laugh at Ceasar	stabbing	Crowd	Spotter D-7	3		
59				the gods be with Ceasar	give thy brother strength	Crowd	Spotter D-7	3		
60				segue	we are gods!	laughter	Western Elec D-8	2		
61				segue	We are dust	crowd	Spotter D-7	3		
62				Caligula Ceasar)	Men Forget)	crowd	Spotter D-7	3		
63				Caligula Ceasar)	Men Forget)	laughter	Western Elec. D-8	2		
64				Caligula leaves stage	2nd laugh	laughter	Western Elec D-8	2		
65				Segue	Hail Ceasar. Hail to death	crowd	Spotter -D-7	3		
66				Kneel down, Abase yourselves Fear not Caligula! There is no death		Laughter	W.E. D-8	2		
67				Segue	Caligula - hands up	Laughter	W.E. D-8	2		
68				Fool! Madman	Curtain	Orch.	Pit	4 5 6		4 R
69				Segue	End of Orch.	Voice	Booth	1		
70	7	Faust				Margarita	Margarita's monolith	2	6	
71						Mephistofele	Tent	1	18	
72					Curtain up	Organ	Spotter C-9	3		
73						Organ	Spotter C-9			
74						Organ	Spotter C-9			
75						Organ	Spotter C-9			
76						Organ	Spotter C-9			
77										
78										
79					Curtain Down	Chaser	Orch.			
80										

put No	Output Channel Color			Output Control Setting		Speaker Panel Plug	Jack	Speaker Location	Press Next to bottom row of buttons WE 118A Channel Operating Technique
6 7 8	W					4 5 6 7 8	L N H I K	OHSR OHSC OHSL Floor	Start aud. Return 5-8 to white on spk. sub panel. Increase tempo + Intensity thru Jones
2 3	R					1 2 3	E F G	Stand speakers	Form. Fears more from X to Y to Z increasing in Intensity — Kill on Shot
						4 5 6 7 8	L N H I K		Last 13 Drum increase in intensity To maximum.
2 3	R R G					1 2 3	A B C	Procenium	End of Jones Change Input Z to W. E.T.T. to G
						on orch. shift 4 5 6	H I J		
2 3	R					1 2 3	L M N	OHSR OHSC OHSC	On end of chant shift to house speakers
4 5 6 7	R G					2 4 5 6 7 8	H I J 10	Exp HW HE Bal Pit.	lift spotter Spot
									Fade in on Laz. in pit and then fill house
									Spot
									fade crowd fade laughter enough to hear actors
									Spot
									fade Lazarus laughter
									Fade up Lazarus laughter in pit and then fill house.
									fade crowd
									bring up Crowd
									fade laughter
						shift 8 to E			snap down crowd
									bring up crowd
									bring up laughter in pit and then fill house
									fade laughter fast
									Strike Spotter
									Spot W.E. near end of Laughter disc to mark. Start in pit → EH → WH
									↳ fade out laughter strike W.E.
2 3	R W G					1 2 3	A B C	Procenium	
5 6	W					2 4 5 6	B H I J	Exp. WH EH Bal.	
5	W	8	10 10			4 5	H I	WH EH Bal	Margarita's Mike (plugged in during VOLP
8	G	26				8	E	Stg. R.	Mephis Test Mike
2 3	R					1 2 3	L M N	OHSR OHSC OHSL	
						1 2 3	A B C	PR PC PL	

It is recommended that the sound technician, before he begins operation, read the pertinent publications listed in the bibliography and the tape recorder manufacturer's instruction manual for the selected machine. Indexing of the manual, including the affixing of subject tabs, is recommended. After the information in the operating manual has been absorbed, the sound technician can begin experimental recording to familiarize himself with the equipment.

TAPE

The first step is to select the tape to use. Each of the many makes of tapes requires a somewhat different equalization and bias current so it is well to use only the brand of tape recommended by the manufacturer of the recorder. For uniform results, this choice must be adhered to and the same type of tape used consistently. Otherwise the operator may need to readjust bias level and recording equalization with each new batch of tape. Uniformity of recorded level is extremely important, especially when tapes recorded at different times are spliced together to be used in sequence.

After the recorder has been aligned and tested according to the manufacturer's instructions, tapes are checked for uniformity. Each reel of tape is checked for signal intensity by the following procedure:

1. Thread a tape on the machine. Terminate the output with the proper loading resistor (600 ohms on recommended machines) and connect a vacuum-tube voltmeter across this load. Connect an audio oscillator generating a 500 Hz signal to the line input connector and start the machine in the record mode.

2. Switch the record level VU meter to input and adjust signal level to zero. Switch the VU meter to measure the output level from tape. This level should be zero within 1 dB. Set aside one reel of tape most nearly meeting this requirement to serve as a standard in later maintenance checks. Each new batch of tape is checked against this standard. To further ensure uniformity, tape should be purchased in cartons of 12 reels.

In high-quality commercial recording, a tape speed of fifteen inches per second is considered to be the primary standard speed. Seven and one half inches per second is secondary standard. At the higher tape speed, editing is easier and re-recording introduces less distortion. It is therefore recommended that original recordings be made at 15 inches per second and that the final performance tape copied at 7.5 inches per second, to limit the number of reels.

PRINT THROUGH

Print through is the magnetization of adjacent layers in recorded tapes and is heard as a faint echo. At high reproduce levels it can be quite annoying. It can be minimized by the use of tapes having a 1.5 mil base, such as Minnesota Mining and Manufacturing Company's No. 208. Control of the temperature of the storage room to not more than 70 degrees Fahrenheit will help, as tests have shown that print through increases if the tapes are stored in an environment of 80 degrees or higher. Low temperatures and high humidity must be avoided.

ENVIRONMENT

High humidity has a softening effect on acetate tapes. Chilling will adversely affect both tape and mechanism. At temperatures below 60 degrees Fahrenheit there is a tendency for the magnetic coating to loosen from the base, if the tape is flexed over a capstan of small diameter.

High temperatures during operation must also be guarded against. Overheating of the recorder motor in some machines can cause hunting which produces a flutter in the recorded signal. Adequate ventilation is required for the recorder cabinet, especially if a large amount of equipment is assembled in a small operating booth. Blowers can be installed for ventilation, but well-controlled, silent air conditioning will benefit both the equipment and the operator.

EQUIPMENT SETUP

The setup of equipment for a recording session must be planned in detail. After consulting with the director to clarify his objectives, the sound technician will list needed gear and will chart the placement of microphones to get desired results.

All equipment must be set up and operating well in advance of the session. All adjustments are made before the arrival of the cast and director, so that it will not be necessary to fiddle with mechanical and acoustical details while the director boils and fumes. It is a good idea to keep in mind the Hollywood *stand-in* technique in which all measurements and tests are made in the absence of important players.

To prevent distorted tapes, a head demagnetizer is needed. If magnetization of the heads is suspected, the demagnetizer should be used according to manufacturer's instructions.

If at all possible, the recording studio should be located near the auditorium so that loudspeakers, in final playing position, can be used for monitoring. This will allow the director to hear rehearsals in performance volume and perspective.

Microphones are placed to avoid pickup of mechanical noise from the recorder, excessive sibilance in speech, and paper rattle from scripts. Prior to rehearsal the operator should listen, with equipment gain *full*, for possible pickup of broadcast signals. If such signals are picked up, careful grounding of the recorder will usually eliminate them. If not, an r. f. filter may be inserted in the input lines, if the frequency of the interfering station is known. Power lines must not parallel microphone lines.

RECORDING TECHNIQUES

All recordings are made *flat*. If special effects are desired by the director, program equalizers are inserted into the monitoring lines. Settings are carefully noted so that the effect may be recreated for playback and performance. This technique is advised to avoid the introduction of distortion. For instance, excessive high-frequency emphasis can overload the tape even when the overload is not evident on the VU meter or audible in the monitoring system.

Auxiliary equipment for dubbing from disc to tape. Provincial Hall, Edmonton, Alberta.

All fading in and out must be done slowly and smoothly. Low-level background sounds and reverberation—inaudible or not noticed while monitoring—will be brought to the attention of the audience if started or broken off abruptly.

When recording in remote locations, it is well to record several minutes of background sounds without action. If studio retakes are necessary these background sounds can be mixed in, to maintain unity of place.

A number of sounds usually produced by mechanical means can be recorded and kept as a library for use when needed. Rainfall, wind, bells, chimes, factory whistles, and the like can be dubbed from effect discs or recorded from live sources. Telephone bell ringing, for example, may be canned by setting up a microphone near the ringer box after an assistant has dialed the number from another telephone. This will remove a long existing annoyance, where, even in the most professional Broadway productions, the audience hears a doorbell and then sees a well-trained butler answer the telephone.

At all recording sessions, the capstan, pressure roller and all three heads must be examined from time to time, for the accumulation of oxide dust, since recording quality can be affected thereby. Any coating of the listed parts by this red dust should be wiped off, using a cloth moistened slightly with *alcohol*. CAUTION: *Never use carbon tetrachloride*, which even in small quantities will ruin the tape base, or cause slippage in the neoprene friction drives of the mechanism.

EDITING

Editing of recorded tape for the theatre usually consists of the selection of single sounds and the arrangement of these sounds into a sequence to be reproduced on cue. Effective use of these sounds has been covered in other portions of this book. Mechanical details of the editing process will be treated here.

Editing must be performed with care and without distraction. Headphones will provide some isolation from distracting noises but, for best results, an isolated, soundproof room is best.

The tape editor must be able to hear all sounds on the tape if he is to do an effective job. He must use a reproducing system and loudspeaker of very low distortion and noise level. He must operate the reproducing system at a fairly high level, keeping in mind, however, the hazards of hearing fatigue, and the resulting loss in hearing acuity and powers of concentration.

After playing the tape and using a stopwatch to time and locate desired passages, he is ready to begin cutting. His tools are:

Unmagnetized scissors and single-edged razor blades.
Timing tape, Scotch Brand No. 43.
Splicing tape, Scotch brand No. 41, 7/32-inch wide.
A good splicing block.
A black china- or glass-marking crayon.

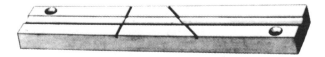

EdiTall tape splicer.

The beginning of the wanted sound is located by the timing method mentioned above. Then the precise point of start is located by running the tape slowly over the heads, turning the tape reels by hand. When the editor is sure that the wanted spot is at the gap in the reproduce head, he makes a small mark on the back of the tape, opposite the gap. He then checks the accuracy of the mark by rewinding the tape for about a foot and then running it at normal speed, observing the coincidence of the sound and the arrival of the mark at the head gap. It is suggested that until he has gained experience the editor make his first cuts in a practice tape.

When the editor is satisfied that sound and mark are in

register, he removes the tape from the head assembly and inserts it, back side up in the splicing block. The tape is slid in the block groove until the crayon mark centers on the 45-degree cutting guide. A ninety degree cut causes a click. Using a backed, single-edge razor blade, he cuts neatly along the guide slot. The unwanted end of the tape is then removed and timing tape previously cut at the appropriate 45-degree angle is inserted in its place. The two ends must be butted neatly together, with no gap, overlap, or buckling. A one-inch length of splicing tape is pressed gently over the joint, centering on it. Care must be taken that the splicing tape does not overlap the edge of the recording tape as it will rub against the recording head and possibly contaminate it with the adhesive material.

The best length of the piece of splicing tape must be found by trial and error. Its length depends on the tape tension maintained by the particular machine, if too long or too short its stiffness may lift the tape away from the reproduce head and cause a *dropout* in the signal. If too short it may also result in an insecure splice.

No setting or drying time is needed for the adhesive material. The spliced tape can be threaded into the machine and played immediately, permitting the editor to check the results of his handiwork. As stated previously, practice is essential. The editor must keep on making and testing splices until he has mastered the technique.

In editing and splicing, several precautions must be taken:

1. Magnetized razor blades or scissors will affect the tape and cause clicks. A head demagnetizer can be used to correct this condition.
2. Timing tape should be white or a very light color so it can be seen easily in a dim light. It must also accept ink cueing marks. Some types of plastic tape cannot be marked and some will even become charged electrostatically and be noisy in passing over the heads.
3. Never use household cellulose tape for splicing or any other purpose near a tape recorder. Its adhesive material will bleed under pressure. Serious damage to recording mechanisms has resulted from the adhesive material being transferred to a critical moving part by the operator's hands.
4. Do not run the tape at fast forward or rewind speeds in contact with the heads. Magnetic tape coating is an abrasive and wearing of the heads results even from normal use. Although the tape tension may be reduced during high-speed operation, wear still results. Remove the tape from contact with the heads at all times when not actually recording or listening.

CUEING

The mechanics of tape cueing depends primarily upon the starting characteristics of the tape transport mechanism. A delay occurs between switch action and response. The delay differs between makes of machines but is shortest in those

which bring the tape into contact with a constantly turning capstan and longest in those which start by switching electric power to the drive motor.

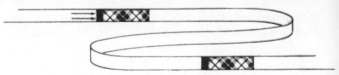

Timing leader tape. (*Minnesota Mining and Manufacturing Co.*)

To measure this delay a time-marked leader tape is used. The leader tape is marked at ¾-inch intervals, each of which corresponds to $1/10$ second at 7½ inches per second and spliced to the end of a magnetic tape on which a 3000-cycle signal is recorded. The cue mark is located by repeatedly playing the tape, starting operation with the first mark placed at a fixed reference point such as the edge of the head assembly enclosure or the capstan. The length of the leader tape is increased in ¾-inch steps until the start of the sound is clean, without pitch change or flutter.

If the final tape is made up of desired sounds, in sequence, each separated by sections of cue-marked timing tape, accurate, assured cueing is possible. The sound is identified by a descriptive word or a number placed on the timing tape in advance of the cue mark.

A good copy of the final tape must be prepared and held as a standby for emergencies. In extremely critical situations an additional copy is set up on a standby reproducer. This understudy is run through each performance, silent but ready to be switched into the control system should operation of the primary system be interrupted.

CAUTION

Sound control has had a hard time in the theatre, because it has too often been neglected in the planning, and pinched in the budget. Producers have assumed that a backstage electronic installation suitable only for effects could enhance the singing voice, provide movement, and control spatial characteristics and the spectrum of the sound. This is folly. Electronic sound apparatus when operated backstage cannot achieve subtlety. The mechanical prop-effect machines, though limited in power, provided more consistent performance, for they were not required to do more than they could. Electronic amplification, by reason of its great dynamic range, requires precise control not possible backstage.

Also, planning the sound control cannot be undertaken as an enterprise separate from the rest of the production. If the theatrical values in sound are to be most effectively exploited, the sound control must be planned as a part of the whole production. The planning must be done by someone who knows sound and the other elements of production, and who has authority to get it produced as planned.

CHAPTER X

INSTALLATION, OPERATION, AND MAINTENANCE

ELECTRONIC SOUND CONTROL equipment is the most complex and delicate equipment used in the theatre. It requires care in installation, artistry in operation, and thoroughness in maintenance.

PERMANENT INSTALLATIONS

When sound control systems are to be permanently installed as part of a new building, the installation proceeds from plans which should have developed the architectural, acoustical, and electronic elements simultaneously. The electrical contractor lays out and installs all conduit for sound as well as communication, light, and power circuits. The grouping of the elements of the sound system is made more or less rigid by the conduit layout. Since there is usually one best way to achieve simplicity of operation and maintenance, the sound system engineer will have to see to it not only that his loudspeakers are in the right places, but that the electrical contractor's layout does not limit the flexibility of the system by running conduit and locating outlets where they are structurally convenient instead of operationally efficient.

PORTABLE SYSTEMS

Portable systems used in the theatre are built into boxes, constructed in a property shop, similar to those used for lighting equipment. The boxes in which amplifiers, control panels and reproducers are housed serve to protect the equipment from damage, dust, and pilferage. They are caster mounted for easy moving. The equipment can be operated without removal from the box. The boxes can be locked without breaking hookup connections if cable holes are provided.

PERSONNEL

The sound technician may, and in most instances should, rank as a department head though for small simple systems, he may be a member of the electrical department, since his equipment comes under the cognizance of that department. The sound technician may have no assistants for rehearsal or operation but will borrow men normally assigned to lights to help him run cable, move loudspeakers, and test circuits. Similarly, the sound technician will require assistance from the carpenter in installing flown equipment and units which are built into scenery. He will work out with the prop men the location, operation, and cueing procedures for prop sound effects if these are to be picked up by microphone. In such cases (the subsonic drum, the man walking through brush) sound technicians will have to be responsible for performance by a property man over whom tradition and standard organizational practice give him no authority. The best way to insure a smooth show under these circumstances is to have a prop man who is young enough to learn and a stage manager who understands something about sound.

ASSEMBLY PROCESS

The bring-in and assembly are in the best of circumstances simultaneous, with numerous items onstage in place before the last of the show arrives in the alley. Sound control equipment is handled with and at the same time as the electrical equipment and follows the same general procedure and time schedule in assembly. The amplifiers and control consoles are taken to operating position at about the same time the switchboard is being set up. Spotlines for microphone enclosures, tents, and backstage loudspeakers are rigged while the lights are going onto the first pipe. In point of fact, it is a question of availability of manpower more than the space limitation that governs the order in which electrical and sound elements are set up. The sound technician will find it to his advantage to get the power line out to his equipment as soon as possible so that he can hook up one circuit. This has many advantages. First, he can set up a microphone on a floor stand onstage and feed any available loudspeaker and then tell the carpenter he may use the system to help him rig the show. This helps the carpenter and also makes it possible for the sound technician to test out circuit after circuit without interfering with assembly operations, and nobody complains that the sound system interferes with his work.

While the sets go up, it is quite difficult to work onstage. That is the time the sound technician rigs his front-house loudspeakers, runs his cable out front, and tests circuits.

LOCATION OF EQUIPMENT

Where a sound control booth is available or can be improvised, cable to loudspeakers, microphones, and the power cable (if the A.C. main is backstage) are best run in the loft above the house ceiling. Microphone cables must be kept away from the others, preferably on the other side of the house.

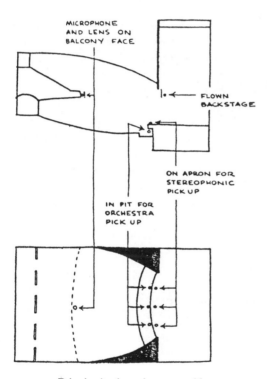

MICROPHONE
AND LENS ON
BALCONY FACE

FLOWN
BACKSTAGE

ON APRON FOR
STEREOPHONIC
PICK UP

IN PIT FOR
ORCHESTRA
PICK UP

Principal microphone positions.

Where loudspeakers or microphones are flown or are built into flown equipment, the cables can often run from above the house to the fly gallery or to the gridiron and thence, with adequate slack, to the end of the batten or to the spot line on which the unit is rigged. Thus flown units can be permanently hooked up to the control system.

To keep cable off the stage floor it is often feasible to carry lines to set or rolling units through the trap room to the playing position and terminating them in connectors, brought up through traps or lighting pockets. The electrician who hooks up the unit in place during the shift will then not need to lay out a line of cable which might be a bother or a hazard on the floor.

TEST PROCEDURES

The sound technician must be available to direct the placement of loudspeakers or microphones into sets as they are assembled onstage. In a well-planned show special toggles and braces will have been provided in the shop. However, the wiring must be applied and secured for all elements that remain assembled for the run, and continuity tests must be made before units which work stage center are flown or run to stored position if this is at all possible. Time is hard to come by and it is often not feasible to dig a wing out of a stack or bring in a back wall to run a continuity test. On flown units it is important wherever possible to rig the cable so that connections will not need to be broken when the unit is taken out.

During assembly the sound technician can test all circuits for continuity and get a fair idea of the performance of his equipment. He has to make a number of other tests not all of which can be accomplished at any one time, but must be made when the theatre is quiet, usually after the crews leave for the night. Once his equipment is rigged, the sound technician works while the others sleep except for rehearsals involving sound as well as other departments. His first concern is to see that the system does not make a noise.

HUM

The first recommendation in connecting microphones into the sound control system is that there shall be but one ground. Since there are stray currents flowing through earth, a second ground on a microphone cable at some distance from the system will usually result in some of these earth currents being conducted into the signal wires, amplified and so reproduced in the speaker as noise. Care must also be taken that microphone wires do not parallel power-carrying cables because magnetically induced pick-up may result. A shield over the cable will prevent electrostatic pickup but not electromagnetic or inductive pick-up. Hum in the power amplifiers may be minimized by following manufacturer's instructions for hum balance if required. The simplest check is, of course, the ear, but a practicable check is to connect an electronic voltmeter or oscilloscope across the loaded output line while testing for hum.

DISTORTION

The proximity of certain kinds of electrical equipment will introduce distortion into the signal. A substation for the New York subway located near the former Hammerstein Theatre introduced distortion into a system installed in that theatre to the extent that audio oscillator signals examined on the oscilloscope were square. Extensive relocation of the lines eliminated this distortion.

NOISE

After the lights are all rigged, it is necessary to run through all the sounds in the show at a level considerably higher than is to be used, to find rattling gelatin frames. Sometimes the lighting instruments, silent through the rest of the performance, will always rattle and buzz at a specific point in one musical number. Gelatins must be secured against rattle by friction tape binding on the frames or by wedges, and these must be renewed every time the gelatins are replaced.

POWER

Power amplifiers are always tested at full power and balanced for equal output. Since, as previously indicated, an audience soaks up a lot of sound, it is necessary to test the system for output. A theatre of a million cubic feet may need 500 electrical watts or more to achieve a 100-dB level depending on the amount of absorption in the house and stage and the efficiency of the loudspeakers. 1500 watts is not too much in the Philadelphia Academy of Music. With the same loudspeakers similarly placed it is more than you need in Carnegie Hall.

CUEING

An essential part of the assembly is the cueing system. If a telephone or intercom is used for cueing, the operator's receiver will have to be a filtered loudspeaker since he must not wear a head set during operation and what goes on at his position can often be heard by the audience. The combination cue light and telephone with the telephone required only in emergencies is perhaps most satisfactory. The amount of cueing required by the sound system operator is small. He takes his cues from the performance—the orchestra in opera, the band in the circus, business and lines in the legitimate theatre.

A safety measure which is quite important is a red light at each offstage microphone position. Such a light can be installed in the microphone tent or hung above the enclosure. The light is controlled by the sound operator, and is turned on when the microphone is live. It has the effect of keeping people quiet in the general area and of reassuring the actor that he is not talking into a dead microphone. Electrical wiring for this light must not parallel the microphone line.

SHIFTS

Under ideal circumstances sound equipment can be so rigged that none of it needs to be handled during the show. However, when loudspeakers or microphones are built into props or set pieces which are not flown, it is necessary to make the connections after each unit is in position, and break them before the set is struck. This requires one man onstage. It is usually possible to run cables so that one man can do all the jobs necessary for the shift. As a part of the shift it is necessary to work out a system whereby the lines can be tested after the hookup is made. In the case of microphones this is simple since the operator can pick up ambient noise on his VU meter or monitor. To test the loudspeaker he may have to put a signal on the line which the electrician onstage can hear when he makes the hookup and report back to the operator out front by cue or telephone.

Where prop sound sources are to be used with microphone pickup, it is important that they be so located that it will not be necessary to move them or the microphone. When visual or line cues are not necessary, such arrangements should be operated away from the stage in the trap room, prop room, or an unused dressing room.

Prior to technical rehearsal the sound technician settles cues with the stage manager and works out with the carpenter, property man, and electrician the sequence of operations involved in the shifts as they may affect his department, as, for example, the point in the shift the sound man onstage moves a rolling speaker unit from storage to working position, whether or not he waits for a certain element to be brought in before he hooks it up if that is necessary, and so on.

RUN-THROUGH

Once the system is tested in position it is necessary to go through the show cue by cue, and test each sound or sound sequence with a stage manager or assistant stage manager substituting for the performers at microphone locations. The importance of going through cue by cue is that such a run-through will establish the operating procedure as well as demonstrating the sound in more or less the fashion called for. The sound technician can then proceed to fill in his operation sheet, listing the loudspeaker combinations, tentative settings on the equalizing networks and other items which he was not able to establish conclusively in the planning. Several run-throughs will probably be necessary, at least one with the director present, to get the sound ready for the technical rehearsal.

OPERATING TECHNIQUE

A flexible sound control system can be operated in a number of ways to get the same result. Remote input control from a seat in the audience works well where little or no movement is required of the apparent sound source. In practice operating from an output panel has appeared to provide the greater facility.

Since the setup sheet is so laid out that settings are made during lulls between periods of activity, the input panel can be used for pre-setting. Levels are set and channel selector keep depressed on this panel; at warning the proper channel selector key on the output panel is depressed and on cue the attenuator for the selected loudspeaker is raised.

If the desired sound is to be reproduced by a number of loudspeakers, channel master controls can be used. However, since there is a great variation in successive groupings of cues which may be encountered, no hard-and-fast rule for general operation can be laid down.

In arranging the operation sheet, for pre-setting during lulls, all manual operations are rehearsed slowly. The system has been designed to be sufficiently flexible that should one operating routine lead to a mishap, such as microphone feedback, input controls can be reset during this rehearsal and gain limited so that feedback levels are never reached during performance.

TECHNICAL REHEARSAL

The technical rehearsal does not work against the timing restrictions involved in performance. The sound technician has plenty of time to set up each operation from his setup sheet which is, of course, too complex to use in running a show. Any changes in operating procedure or technique which he may make at the technical rehearsal he must immediately record as changes in the setup sheet where he is not likely to forget them, or operating sheets made from the setup sheet will be in error. At the technical rehearsal the floor markings are checked for position and orientation of instruments on stage. In particular, the technical rehearsal demonstrates the feasibility of presetting during lulls in the sound system operation. After the technical rehearsal the sound technician will often have to re-edit the magnetic tape, changing and substituting numbers, and changing timing marks. This process often goes on right through opening.

OPERATING SHEET

After the technical rehearsal has been successfully accomplished—and it may take several—the sound technician will draw operating sheets from his setup sheet. The operating sheet may be a simple standard cue sheet or it may be an annotated script or possess any degree of complexity between these two extremes. Operating from a script, even though the show is not complex, can be an exhausting procedure at least until the show has run a while. If the operator is the musician, as in the case of PROMETHEUS, he will annotate his script which contains also the score and the sound-operation procedure. If he is the conductor, as in the case of THE MOTHER, he will annotate his conductor's score and operate from that.

DRESS REHEARSAL

After technical rehearsal and before dress rehearsal the sound technician will need to work out each element involving the orchestra with the orchestra, and those involving the actors with the actors. Actors will need instructions as to the microphone technique required. A good rule is never to allow the speaker or singer to approach the microphone closer than an arm's length. It is sometimes wise to mark the performer's position on the floor. It is a great help if on the first try when an actor speaks into a microphone in an offstage enclosure a record can be made so that the actor may listen to a playback of his own performance. Modification of the actor's delivery and technique can thus be accomplished in a very short time. If the sound technician and the director try to explain desired changes without a recording, the desired improvements may take considerably longer to accomplish. This same procedure for teaching microphone technique applies to offstage orchestras, some musicians, and the operators of prop sounds picked up by microphone. In case of an orchestra in the pit or away from the stage, the microphone position and orientation must be finally established and steps taken to see that they do not vary. The position of chairs is marked on the floor, and microphones must be hung in fixed positions. It is also important that the conductor understand that after a satisfactory run-through of the musical numbers has been accomplished, he must not change the position of any instruments nor change personnel without another run-through with the sound. Sound needs more rehearsal than any other technical element of the show because it is, in fact, the voice of the actor and the instrument of the musician. It is therefore important that adequate rehearsal time be assigned to it. And this rehearsal time should, in a complex show, be about equivalent to that of all the other technical elements combined. Generally speaking, sound rehearsals should be scheduled as special rehearsals taking place immediately after rehearsal of other elements of production at a time when no other activity is scheduled in the theatre. A good principle to observe which will save considerable time in the total preparation of the show is to allow a day between technical and dress rehearsals during which the sound technician can make necessary changes and test them with actors, musicians, and other people concerned.

———————————————————————▶

Section from the Sound Control Operating Sheet for PRO-METHEUS by Aeschylus. English translation by Edith Hamilton, score by Walter Teschan, produced at the Yale University Theatre. Control was at the Novachord. In this production, speech by the actors was accompanied by background sounds of a musical nature but not suggestive of any conventional musical instrument.

FOUR DESCENDING CHORDS

Large notes struck first, followed immediately by the intervening small notes.

WAVE MOTIF

Glissandi, beginning about an octave above the lowest note, and run rather slowly with increasing swell until the top (about an octave above Middle C) is reached, then two marked diminishes of the swell, to a complete fade and cut. (Rhythm: introductory measures of Schubert's Erlkönig...first nine notes, with a marked slowing of notes 8 and 9.)

SHORT, SUSTAINED UP GLISSANDO:

A glissando, approximately an octave up from the lowest note, running to about high C, representing the sound of the rushing winds in a cave. Sustain pedals both down. Fairly rapid and held until the end of: "...have sped us on to you."

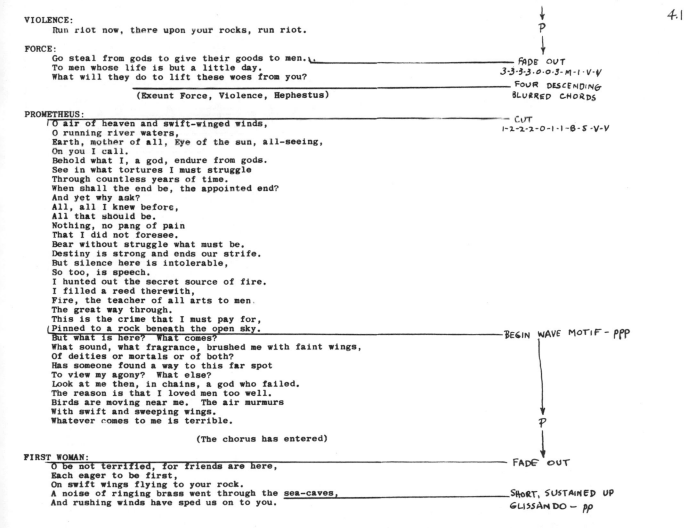

VIOLENCE:
  Run riot now, there upon your rocks, run riot.

FORCE:
  Go steal from gods to give their goods to men.
  To men whose life is but a little day.
  What will they do to lift these woes from you?

(Exeunt Force, Violence, Hephestus)

PROMETHEUS:
  O air of heaven and swift-winged winds,
  O running river waters,
  Earth, mother of all, Eye of the sun, all-seeing,
  On you I call.
  Behold what I, a god, endure from gods.
  See in what tortures I must struggle
  Through countless years of time.
  When shall the end be, the appointed end?
  And yet why ask?
  All, all I knew before,
  All that should be.
  Nothing, no pang of pain
  That I did not foresee.
  Bear without struggle what must be.
  Destiny is strong and ends our strife.
  But silence here is intolerable,
  So too, is speech.
  I hunted out the secret source of fire.
  I filled a reed therewith,
  Fire, the teacher of all arts to men.
  The great way through.
  This is the crime that I must pay for,
  Pinned to a rock beneath the open sky.
  But what is here? What comes?
  What sound, what fragrance, brushed me with faint wings,
  Of deities or mortals or of both?
  Has someone found a way to this far spot
  To view my agony? What else?
  Look at me then, in chains, a god who failed.
  The reason is that I loved men too well.
  Birds are moving near me. The air murmurs
  With swift and sweeping wings.
  Whatever comes to me is terrible.

(The chorus has entered)

FIRST WOMAN:
  O be not terrified, for friends are here,
  Each eager to be first,
  On swift wings flying to your rock.
  A noise of ringing brass went through the sea-caves,
  And rushing winds have sped us on to you.

4.1
↓
P

—— FADE OUT
3-3-3-3-0-0-3-M-1-V-V

—— FOUR DESCENDING
BLURRED CHORDS

— CUT
1-2-2-2-0-1-1-B-S-V-V

— BEGIN WAVE MOTIF - PPP
↓
P
↓

— FADE OUT

— SHORT, SUSTAINED UP
GLISSANDO - pp

Theoretically, the dress rehearsal should proceed without hitch and so far as sound is concerned it sometimes does. However, in general, the director will require some changes in the sound after each dress rehearsal such as change in level, change in timing, or change in operating technique, i.e., rate of crescendo or diminuendo, position of moving sound source with relationship to a line, or some other element of production. It is the precise and artistic use of such subtleties that justifies electronic control of sound, and too much attention cannot be devoted to them.

CAUTION

Auditory fatigue is a phenomenon few people recognize. The exceedingly short span of auditory memory is also seldom appreciated. These two phenomena combine to make it useless to repeat subtle sound sequences more than a dozen times at a sitting, or to prolong a sound rehearsal or run-through beyond the normal running time of the show.

PREVIEW

The more previews the better. The first thing an audience does is to absorb a lot of sound which will mean that all reference levels established in rehearsals must be revised upward about 5 dB. In some houses 10 to 12 dB additional are required to handle an audience. Also, operating procedure can usually be simplified with each performance of the show for a period of some weeks.

PRE-INSTALLATION TESTS

All equipment is tested immediately upon delivery. After successful inspection for visible shipping damage, units are placed on the test bench and checked electrically. Power amplifiers, after installation of proper bridging transformers, are set up as shown in Test Diagram A, and are checked for power output and gain with controls turned fully clockwise. Required test instruments are:

1. 16-ohm 100-watt terminating resistor.
2. Audio oscillator.
3. Electronic voltmeter (VTVM).

Output power check procedure:

1. Connect 16-ohm terminating resistor to 16-ohm output terminals.

Page from Sound Control Operating Sheet from THE MOTHER produced at the Juilliard School of Music. Operation was by the conductor of the orchestra in the pit.

TEST DIAGRAM A

2. Connect electronic voltmeter across terminating resistor.
3. Connect audio oscillator to bridging input terminals of amplifier.
4. Turn on oscillator and amplifiers.
5. Set audio oscillator for a signal of 1000 Hz.
6. Increase audio oscillator output until VTVM indicates:

    22.0 volts for a 30-watt amplifier.
    23.7 volts for a 35-watt amplifier.
    28.3 volts for a 50-watt amplifier.
    33.5 volts for a 70-watt amplifier.
    40 volts for a 100-watt amplifier.

If the amplifier output does not reach these voltages, rebalance output stage and retest. If voltage readings are not improved, the unit should be returned to the vendor.

GAIN CHECK

If correct output voltages are attained, let the setup stand except for the electronic voltmeter (VTVM) which is reconnected across the input terminals. At full gain setting, input signal should not be more than 1.7 volts.

LINE AND MICROPHONE AMPLIFIERS

Line and microphone amplifiers are set up for test as shown in Test Diagram B.

Required test instruments are:

1. 620-ohm 2-watt terminating resistor.
2. Audio oscillator.
3. Electronic voltmeter.

Output power test procedure:

1. Connect 620-ohm resistor across 600-ohm output terminals.
2. Connect electronic voltmeter across 620-ohm terminating resistor.
3. Connect audio oscillator to amplifier 600-ohm input terminals.

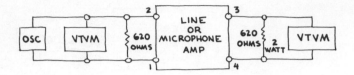

TEST DIAGRAM B

4. Turn on oscillator and amplifier power supplies.
5. Set audio oscillator for a signal of 1000 Hz.
6. Increase audio oscillator output until electronic volt-meter indicates:

    1.23 volts for a 4-dBm amplifier.
    1.54 volts for a 6-dBm amplifier.
    6.15 volts for an 18-dBm amplifier.
    7.75 volts for a 20-dBm amplifier.
    12.3 volts for a 24-dBm amplifier.
    24.5 volts for a 30-dBm amplifier.

GAIN TEST PROCEDURE

If correct output voltages are attained, let the setup stand, except for the electronic voltmeter which is reconnected across the input terminals. Read input voltage and compare with previously read output voltage. Divide the output voltage by the input voltage.

The proper ratios between these two voltages are:

    100/1 for a 40-dB amplifier.
    126/1 for a 42-dB amplifier.
    178/1 for a 45-dB amplifier.
    224/1 for a 47-dB amplifier.
    361/1 for a 50-dB amplifier.
    562/1 for a 53-dB amplifier.

POWER AMPLIFIER PHASE TEST

Power amplifiers are set up for phase relationship tests as shown in Test Diagram C. This test is useless unless bridging transformers are furnished as part of the unit or have been installed with careful attention to uniformity of connections.

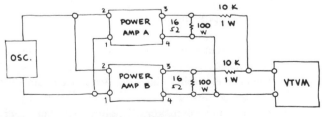

TEST DIAGRAM C

Test procedure:
1. Connect a 16-ohm 100-watt terminating resistor across the 16-ohm output of each two power amplifiers.
2. Connect the 10,000-ohm series resistors to the electronic voltmeter as shown in the diagram.
3. Connect audio oscillator and resistor network as shown in diagram.
4. Turn amplifier gain controls off, fully counter clock-wise.
5. Turn on both amplifiers.
6. Set audio oscillator for a signal of 1000 Hz. Turn output control to minimum.
7. Advance gain control of amplifier No. 1 to a point about halfway between OFF and FULL.
8. Increase audio oscillator output until the electronic voltmeter shows a center-scale indication between 1 and 10 volts.
9. Slowly advance gain control of amplifier No. 2.
10. Observe reading on electronic voltmeter.

If the reading on the electronic voltmeter increases after the gain control of amplifier No. 2 reaches the same position as that of the control on No. 1, the two amplifiers are in phase. If the reading dips, the amplifiers are out of phase.
Remedies for out of phase conditions:

    (a) Check test setup for error in input and output terminal connections.
    (b) Compare connection installation of bridging transformers for reversed leads.
11. If no setup or transformer wiring errors are discovered, set aside amplifier No. 2, continuing the test until all other power amplifiers have been checked against No. 1.
12. Tag amplifiers "in phase" or "out of phase" according to their agreement with amplifier No. 1.
13. Reverse input wiring internally on the minority group of amplifiers.

LINE AND MICROPHONE AMPLIFIER PHASE TEST

Line amplifiers are compared in phase with other line amplifiers. Microphone amplifiers are compared with other microphone amplifiers. This test is predicated on the condition that all line amplifiers are of the same make and model and that all microphone amplifiers are of the same make and model. Setup is shown in Test Diagram D.

Test Procedure:
1. Connect a 620-ohm 2-watt resistor across the 600-ohm output terminal of each of two amplifiers.

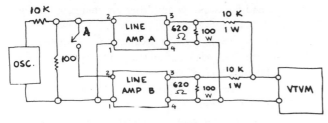

TEST DIAGRAM D

2. Connect 10,000-ohm series resistor to the electronic voltmeter as shown on the diagram.

3. Connect audio oscillator, resistor network, and switch A as shown in Diagram D.

4. Turn on audio oscillator and amplifier power supplies.

5. Set oscillator for a signal of 1000 Hz. Turn output control to minimum.

6. Open switch A.

7. Increase oscillator output until electronic voltmeter shows a center scale reading between 0.1 and 1 volt.

8. Close switch A.

9. A dip in the electronic voltmeter reading indicates an out of phase condition.

10. Proceed as in 11, 12, and 13 of power-amplifier phase test.

11. Reconnect microphone amplifier input for 50 ohms.

LOUDSPEAKER PHASE TEST

As in the case of amplifiers, loudspeakers must be operated *in* phase. Cones or diaphragms must move in the same direction when electrical impulses of the same polarity are applied.

Test procedure:

1. Set two enclosed loudspeakers side by side on the stage apron facing the same direction (toward the house).

2. Connect microphone into microphone amplifier and connect electronic voltmeter as shown in Test Diagram E.

3. Set the microphone facing the loudspeakers on a level with and two feet equidistant from each.

4. Connect the loudspeakers in parallel to a power am-

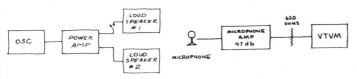

TEST DIAGRAM E

plifier using cables and connectors previously checked for uniform polarity. Open switch A.

5. Impress an audio oscillator signal of 100 Hz through the power amplifier until a tone of moderate loudness is heard from the loudspeakers.

6. Set the electronic voltmeter to its lowest A.C. scale.

7. Increase the oscillator output to get a reading on the electronic voltmeter.

8. Close switch A.

9. A dip in the meter reading indicates an out of phase condition.

10. Tag speaker No. 2 "in phase" or "out of phase" according to result of test.

11. Repeat the test substituting other loudspeakers for No. 2 until all have been checked.

12. Tag all loudspeakers as in 10.

13. Reverse leads at the loudspeaker enclosure connectors in the minority group.

MICROPHONE PHASE TEST

Setup of the test is shown in Test Diagram F.

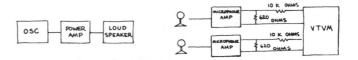

TEST DIAGRAM F

Test procedure:

1. Connect up audio oscillator, power amplifier, and loudspeaker as shown in the diagram.

2. Connect two microphones separately into two microphone amplifiers previously tested and phased.

3. Place microphones side by side and facing loudspeaker at a distance of one foot.

4. Connect the microphone amplifiers to electronic voltmeter as shown in the diagram.

5. Set oscillator at 100 Hz.

6. Turn on oscillator and all amplifiers.

7. Bring up oscillator output until a moderate tone is heard.

8. Set electronic voltmeter on lowest A.C. scale.

9. Disconnect microphone No. 2.

10. Bring up oscillator output until a reading is observed on the electronic voltmeter.

11. Reconnect microphone No. 2.

12. A dip in the electronic voltmeter reading indicates an out-of-phase condition.

13. Tag microphone No. 2 "in phase" or "out of phase" according to result of test.

14. Test all microphones against microphone No. 1 repeating procedure used with No. 2.
15. Reverse connections of the minority group of microphones at output terminals.

CABLES AND CONNECTORS

After connectors have been attached, all cables, interconnecting, microphone, and loudspeaker are rung out for continuity and polarity. An ohmmeter will be needed for this test.

INSTALLATION CHECKOUT

Instruments needed:
Electronic voltmeter with decibel calibration.
Audio oscillator.
Terminating resistors, 100-watt, of proper resistance value for power-amplifier loading:

1. Turn on power and allow system to warm up.
2. Check for amplifier hum as outlined in section on hum.
3. Set up gain and frequency test as shown in Test Diagram G.
4. Adjust audio oscillator for an output of 1000 Hz at 0.8 volt.
5. Transfer electronic voltmeter to power amplifier terminating resistor.
6. Increase gain until voltages shown on electronic voltmeter indicate that the half-power point has been reached.

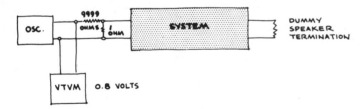

TEST DIAGRAM G

These voltages are 70.7 percent of full output voltage. For a 16-ohm termination they are:

15.5   volts for a 30-watt amplifier.
16.7   volts for a 35-watt amplifier.
20.0   volts for a 50-watt amplifier.
24.00   volts for a 70-watt amplifier.
28.28   volts for a 100-watt amplifier (use a 200-watt terminating resistor).

7. Set and fix all power amplifier internal gain settings for these voltages.
8. Without changing test setup, run a frequency response check of all channels and all amplifiers, using following procedure:
   (a) Use constant output of approximately 10 volts.
   (b) Vary input to get this output.
   (c) Check in half octave steps from 25 Hz to 16,000 Hz.
9. Note input levels in decibels in relation to level at 1000 Hz. Reverse signs for correct response.
10. Insert fixed equalizers (microphone and phonograph) and repeat 7 and 8.
11. Compare resulting response with NAB (RIAA) standard curve and microphone response curve furnished by manufacturer.
12. Re-connect loudspeakers.
13. Check each loudspeaker at half its power by sweeping through full frequency range, to detect resonances in enclosure and nearby objects.

PRE-PERFORMANCE CHECK

1. Remove dust covers.
2. Disconnect and then reconnect all low-level connectors (microphone and line) to clean contacts.
3. Turn on power, allow equipment to warm up.
4. Set controls to highest operating point and listen for hum and tube noise.
5. Test microphones and circuits by speaking into each.
6. Run a test signal through each circuit.
7. With this test signal, test each loudspeaker at full volume for rattle of nearby lamps, gelatin frames, or other objects.
8. Operate all controls for noise.
9. Make necessary adjustments and replacements.
10. Test cue and communication system.
11. Set up for performance.

START-OF-SEASON CHECKOUT

1. Uncover all switches and controls.
2. Clean contacts with contact cleaner (except at tape recorder). (see note under that heading.)
3. Clean all connector contacts, using buffing wheel if corrosion is evident.
4. Proceed with checkout, using procedures 1 to 13 inclusive of installation checkout.
5. Lubricate moving mechanisms (disc reproducers and tape recorders) exactly as advised by manufacturer's manuals.

BIBLIOGRAPHY

Bartholomew, Wilmer T., *Acoustics of Music,* Prentice Hall, Inc., New York, 1942.

Burris-Meyer, Harold, and Cole, Edward C., *Theatres and Auditoriums,* Robert E. Krieger Publishing Co. Inc., Huntington, New York, 2nd edition with supplement, 1975. *Scenery for the Theatre,* Little Brown and Co., Boston, 2nd edition, 1971.

Burris-Meyer, Harold, and Goodfriend, Lewis S., *Acoustics for the Architect,* Robert E. Krieger Publishing Co. Inc., Hunginton, New York.

Collison, David, *Stage Sound,* Drama Book Specialists, New York, 1976.

Davis, Hallowell, *Hearing and Deafness,* Murray Hill Books, Inc., New York, 1947.

Knudsen, Vern O., and Harris, Cyril M., *Acoustical Designing in Architecture,* John Wiley & Sons, Inc., New York, 1950.

Olson, Harry F., *Modern Sound Reproduction,* Van Nostrand Reinhold Co., New York, 1972.

Roederer, Julian C., *Introduction to the Physics and Psychophysics of Music,* Springer Verlag, New York, 1973.

Stevens, S. S., and Davis, Hallowell, *Hearing, Its Psychology and Physiology,* John Wiley & Sons, Inc., New York, 1938.

Wasser Carol, *Sound and Music for the Theatre,* Richards Rosen Press, New York, 1976.

PERIODICALS

Journal of the Acoustical Society of America, American Institute of Physics, New York.

Journal of the Audio Engineering Society, New York.

Theatre Design and Technology, U. S. Institute for Theatre Technology, New York.

INDEX